Fox Fotos

JOHN A. STRALEY

is a director of the Dealers' Digest Publishing Company, and Associate Editor of the *Investment Dealers' Digest,* for which he writes the weekly section on investment companies. He serves annually as Manager of the national Mutual Fund Sales Convention.

Mr. Straley is also well known as editor of *The Bawl Street Journal,* the humorous newspaper published each June which satirizes the world of finance.

What About Mutual Funds?

WHAT ABOUT
MUTUAL FUNDS?

By John A. Straley

Associate Editor, *Investment Dealers' Digest*

Illustrations by Stephen J. Voorhies

REVISED EDITION

HARPER & BROTHERS   NEW YORK

Contents

Preface

This book is designed to help men and women who would like to become investors but have not the time, nor the facts necessary, to choose among the thousands of stocks and bonds they might buy. They would also find it difficult, or at least inconvenient, to keep track of and judge the many influences which might affect securities after they are bought.

Readers will find that such things are done automatically through ownership of open-end investment companies, or mutual funds. The professional managers of funds select securities, watch them, and change them when necessary, bringing to that work years of experience. Mutual funds provide a convenient way to own a cross section in, and share in the profits of, the great industries which are the backbone of America.

The author has been identified with mutual funds for over twenty-five years. He has traveled from coast to coast organizing and managing conventions of investment dealers ranging in size from 400 to over 1600 people. He has talked with private investors in all walks of life, and answered their questions about the modern, practical form of owning many securities in one known as the mutual fund.

In this book the reader will find set forth in an interesting, informal way just what such companies are and what the investor may expect from them. This second edition retains some examples of investment management at work which, while not recent, still effectively illustrate the points discussed. Otherwise, the original text has been updated and supplemented by later material.

JOHN A. STRALEY

New York City
June 15, 1958

1. You—and Mutual Funds

How can mutual funds help you?—Do well-informed investors buy them?—What do they offer you?—Mutual funds defined—How they are put together—Why not just buy the same stocks yourself?

A nice young American had lost his last cent at Monte Carlo, and went back to his hotel room to shoot himself. As he raised the gun to his head he heard a mysterious Little Voice say to him, "Look under your shoe."

Stuck to the sole of his shoe he found a $1,000 bill, and the Little Voice said, "Go back to the Casino."

Back at the gaming table he heard the Little Voice say, "Play thirteen," which he did, and thirteen promptly came up, after which he followed the mysterious advisor for six more straight wins. By this time he had amassed quite a fortune, and the Little Voice excitedly whispered, "Double zero. Bet the works."

He did, but double zero did not come up, at which the Little Voice disgustedly muttered, "Oh, nuts!"

What every investor would love is a sort of financial Little Voice, errorproof, of course, to tell him what securities to buy and sell, and more important, when to do so. But Little Voices, particularly the kind that are never wrong, are not usually available. The nearest the investor can come to such a source of information is to be guided by professional investment counsel.

What makes this impractical is that there just is not enough capable investment counsel to go around, plus the fact that fees for such counsel are far beyond the reach of most investors. Investment counsel firms can rarely afford to set up a custom-made account with less than $100,000 of principal, and even on these "small" accounts the annual fee would be at least 1 per cent.

Here is a typical investment counsel approach:

Many people who accumulate securities to produce extra income, or to act as a support in their old age, make their investments with no plan, and no real objective. As a result, while each security owned may have elements of yield, marketability, and perhaps even a chance of gain, no two are in any way related nor is the list as a whole designed to assure, for that particular investor, the special goals his individual circumstances demand.

This "Alice in Wonderland" investing—buying securities because they are recommended by a well-meaning friend, or represent some industry currently favorably in the public eye, or which "did well last year"—may temporarily appear successful, but will not and cannot be as rewarding as a planned program designed to meet particular needs.

That is a fine approach, and a sound one, but unless your circumstances are unusual you can probably get your quota of capable, experienced investment management by owning shares in a *mutual fund*. If you do, you will have plenty of good company. Trust accounts, colleges, hospitals, charitable foundations, labor unions, lodges, churches, and almost any sort of organization you can name will be found on the shareholders' lists of not all, but many mutual funds.

A concrete tribute to the philosophy of equity investment under professional management was paid in 1948 by Harvard University, whose endowment fund of over $500,960,000 is one of the world's largest, when after operating the account themselves for many years they turned it over to a management identified with a mutual fund.

More recently, in New York State, the 130 savings banks decided that they should have a mutual fund to simplify for them their problems of choosing and watching their investments in common stocks. They formed Institutional Investors Mutual Fund and more than 60 of the banks have availed themselves of it. There are many strict limits to the percentage of its money a bank may invest in this fund. In 1956, the Connecticut savings banks followed suit.

Probably you have heard your friends talk about mutual funds, just as pleased users talk about any product which is becoming increasingly popular. Officially, there is no such thing as a mutual fund. That is a trade name for what the government calls *open-end investment companies*. These investment companies, or funds, come in many popular models to meet various needs and purposes. Their shares can be bought in modest amounts, or in the larger economy sizes. You can buy them for cash in any desired number, or arrange convenient investments out of your family budget.

Mutual fund shares are readily marketable, perhaps for more than the investor paid, although your dealer or salesman is obligated to tell you that you may receive less than your purchase price. Shares are quoted daily in leading newspapers throughout the United States. They simplify life by allowing more hours for recreation and pleasure.

After your savings bank nest egg and some reasonable amount of insurance have been provided for, take a look at mutual funds and see what they can do for you. This book tells most of the things you should know about them, and describes for you other publications in which you will find interesting and helpful data on investment companies. Also, it will probably suggest to you some questions you may wish to ask the next mutual fund salesman who calls.

You will find nothing profound in this book. Its chapters are simply a series of friendly talks based largely on the answers to questions people have asked the author after his appearances at service clubs, church societies, women's groups, and other gatherings, plus conversations with investment dealers and their clients in homes and offices from coast to coast, as well as in many off-trail spots such as a Michigan chicken farm, a Texas corral, a YMCA swimming pool in Cincinnati, and meetings with investment committees at churches and colleges. Basically, the questions asked boil down to three:

1. Will my money be safe?
2. What income will I receive?
3. Can I get out, if I want to?

Along with these, there follow two related questions.

1. When I get out, how much will I receive?
2. Will these shares protect me against the continuing rise in living costs?

There is an old saying which goes, "When someone tells you of the great things he will do tomorrow, ask what he did yesterday." As Benjamin Franklin put it: "No light guides us to the future like that illumining our path from the past." Complete records of mutual fund performance, and what they have paid out to shareholders, are available from your dealer. So are figures on how living costs have changed.

In any investment "safety" is a relative term. If you mean, "Will I get back the number of dollars I put in?" or "Will I receive a guaranteed number of dollars at some future date?" your mutual fund dealer will make no prophecies. Results from holdings in a fund are not restricted to fixed numbers of dollars. They may be less than you had hoped, or more.

As to income, it will vary according to the fund you invest in, and what business conditions are, somewhat as it might vary if you owned 10, or 50, or 100 individual stocks or bonds. The liquidating provision that shares in a mutual fund may be presented for redemption on any business day should answer the question about getting out. Again, your dealer will tell you that when you sell you may receive either less or more than you paid.

In this book are many other facts to help answer these basic questions, but before we begin our blow-by-blow description of mutual funds let us see what they are and what makes them tick. The mutual fund is the offspring of the free enterprise system. It enables any investor to share in American industry. You are familiar with mutual savings banks, and mutual insurance companies. Mutual funds are not like savings banks or insurance companies, but are designed to act as suitable parts of the growth or risk portion of your investment plan.

A slogan of the mutual fund industry describes them as "Packages of American Earning Power." In a contest run by the *Investment Dealers' Digest* in 1953, calling for "the best description of a mutual fund in 30 words or less," winner of the first prize was:

A mutual fund combines the capital of many investors to employ experienced management in purchasing securities of many companies, thus providing diversification and supervision the investors could not individually afford.

Diversification is a two-dollar word meaning "spreading the risk." No insurance company, or investment company, could exist without it.

Winner of the second prize simplified the matter somewhat by describing a fund as something that "combines in one stock certificate the convenience and satisfaction of owning shares in many industries." This makes a good point. When you buy a cross section of American industry through a fund, you aid and at the same time benefit by the system which encourages free enterprise and private initiative. The fund is a living example of democracy in action—every shareholder enjoys similar rights and receives similar services.

A fund's list of securities owned (what the salesman would call its *portfolio*) is a sort of all-American team. If you stood on a hilltop near a railroad and watched a long freight train pass, there would scarcely be a profitable industry represented by the train (from its slick diesel engine and the steel and electric controls and highly specialized equipment that went into its making) or by the cargo it carried, which would not be found in the securities in which you had an interest. You might see wheat from the Northwest, ore from the Great Lakes region, cattle from the Southwest, Florida or California citrus fruits, chemicals and oils, television sets, a flatcar with new automobiles, electric refrigerators, tractors, coal, cotton, or a host of other products.

As an example of this, get the salesman to show you the portfolio of any good fund. Note the holdings by industries, as well as the companies themselves which are represented. You will be amazed at the number of companies whose products you use every day. You are paying them—why not let them pay you?

With these things in mind, let us suppose you have guests in your home some evening and the talk turns to high living costs, the need for more income to meet higher costs, the general desire to be worth a million dollars, and so on.

Everybody would like to put some money where it will grow, and maybe somebody says wistfully, "I ought to start a margin account, I've made a lot of money playing the stock market on paper."

"On paper, huh?" another neighbor sniffs. "Sounds about as exciting as a good game of strip solitaire."

Finally somebody mentions mutual funds, and there is a general chorus of "What are they? What do they do?"

Suppose there were ten of you, and each put $100 into a basket in the middle of your livingroom floor. Each would then have an equal share in this mutual venture, and an equal vote when matters of policy were to be decided. As you have not made any investments, each share is worth the $100 originally put in. When you divide the worth of the entire assets (the $1,000 you own as a group) by the number of shares (10), you get what is called the *net asset value per share*.

Now, let us go on one step, and assume you folks have bought some securities with your $1,000. They have risen in price and could be sold for $1,100. One of the group has other uses for his money and wants to get out. Again you divide the total worth of your basket of money by the number of shares, and pay off the person who withdraws with the sum of $110. Or, if the securities you owned had declined to a total value of $900 he would get out for the $90 representing his share.

Suppose the Joneses, up the block, hear of this scheme of yours and want to get in on it. If your asset value per share is $110, that is what they would have to pay to buy one share in your group.

So far, we have assumed that all the work in connection with this venture has been done for love. Somebody had to take the responsibility of selecting the securities you bought. Someone had to decide which ones should be kept, and which sold. Too, there was another kind of responsibility—taking physical care of the securities you owned, so that they would be available on demand. In addition to these things, you would have the question of dividing among your group members the bond interest or the dividends on stocks held, so that each member of the group received exactly his or her fair share.

It is easy to see that this venture of yours quickly gets past the "fun" stage. To keep it going means work, real work, for someone.

About at this point in your mutual investment, some member may ask, "Why don't we just buy shares in some good fund, and avoid all this detail?"

"Wait a minute," someone else may say. "It costs money to get into those funds."

"That's right," another may add. "And I hear they charge you something every year, just to watch the securities the fund owns."

Both of these statements are correct, and there are also administrative expenses, usually amounting to something under 0.25% yearly. The management fee for watching the securities ordinarily runs about 0.5% a year. This means that for management, an investor with $10,000 in a fund would be paying something less than the price of a pack of cigarettes per day.

"Seems reasonable enough," one of your group may say, "but what about this cost of getting in and out of a fund? Wouldn't we be better off just to buy some stocks ourselves?"

The important thing to remember about a purchase of mutual fund shares is that you are not buying a stock, but acquiring a service. The getting-in cost, averaging 7.5% of the offering price on small purchases and considerably lower on large ones, usually includes the cost of exit. With a very few exceptions, there is no exit charge. In transactions using groups of individual stocks the percentage of expense would vary widely, because the total in-and-out cost would depend entirely upon how many stocks were bought and how much money went into each.

To get a fair comparison of just what you would pay to *buy and sell* some individual stocks, and how the total cost would compare with the acquisition cost of a fund you are considering, get the individual stock figures from any brokerage firm, and the fund figure from its prospectus, which the salesman must give you when he makes you an offering of shares.

Mutual funds are probably the only merchandise required by law to show the markup between asset value per share and retail prices. It is no secret that other commodities and services make profits too, but new cars do not carry the cost of manufacture on their windshields, nor do insurance policies state in large letters on their front covers just what part of your premium goes into distribution costs.

The acquisition cost of a mutual fund share should be regarded as an initiation fee such as you would pay if you joined a club. If you are going to be around for only a few days, or weeks, you would not join. Mutual fund shares should not be bought for short-term holding. Their purchase may be likened to setting up a flexible living trust.

A compromise method followed by some investors is to subscribe to various printed services supplying market comment, and recommending certain securities for purchase or sale. On this method of economy, an interesting bulletin was sent out in April 1950 by Arthur Wiesenberger, publisher of the annual *Investment Company Manual*, which you will find described later in our Recommended Reading list. He said:

How much money do investors spend on market services? And how much valuable time do they spend reading, digesting, and deciding when to follow whose advice about buying or selling which securities? The cost of these published market services ranges from $50 to $150 a year, and rare indeed are the market letter fans content to buy them one at a time.

For professional and business people, who must assign cash values to their time and budget its disposition accordingly, the time invested in worrying over market letter recommendations adds up to an invisible but very real cost. At a minimum, say, of two hours a week, and at a nominal time valuation of only $5 an hour, allowing for a two-week vacation, 100 hours a year would cost each subscriber $500 a year over and above the cost of each market service subscribed to.

The practical fact is that the real cost of even casual professional or semi-professional supervision of a list of securities has to be at least $1,000 a year. By contrast, investment company shareholders limit their costs to the size of their investments. The smallest holders enjoy the same supervision as the largest. Altogether, investment companies serve the average investor more economically and more efficiently than the average investor can hope to use market services to serve himself.

They tell a story about a man who called on President Calvin Coolidge after his election. Coolidge, for him, was cordial. "I think it only fair," said the visitor as he took his leave, "to tell you I didn't vote for you."

"Well," smiled Coolidge, "somebody did."

Despite the fact that mutual funds are still less widely known than some other forms of investment, hundreds of thousands of somebodies have voted for them during the past decade. Registrations of ownership at the last year end were in the neighborhood of 3,110,400, compared with 672,543 in December 1947, according to the National Association of Investment Companies. This figure does not relate to that produced as a result of spot sampling by the Brookings Institution in 1952, which estimated only 650,000 mutual fund shareholders.

It is likely that the discrepancy is due to duplication of names for two reasons. First, many dealers and investors like to see money divided under different managements so that too many eggs will not be in one basket. Second, because by selecting three funds with different payment dates an investor can receive a dividend check each month, many have made such a division of investments for reasons of convenience.

With this growth in shareholders in mind, let us run briefly over some of the reasons why people buy mutual funds in addition to the spreading of investment risk.

First, people like income. These funds recently had assets of something over $8.7 billion. In 1957 they distributed to shareholders upwards of $320 million of investment income, and an additional $283,451,000 in securities profits. And, although the amounts and percentages paid have varied, no mutual fund has ever missed making a regular scheduled payment from investment income.

Second, shares are easy to buy and sell. Your dealer can tell you the offering price at any time. On any business day, if you wish to do so, you may present your shares for redemption by the fund. You may send them direct, or your dealer can do it for you. Share markets are not based on supply and demand, but on asset values as determined twice on each full business day.

Third, you are entitled to know what your fund is doing. Federal law requires that you receive a prospectus, and that you be sent annual and semiannual reports, independently audited. Most of the funds supply additional information in the form of quarterly reports with lists of their holdings, and all funds give you the figures necessary for tax purposes in reporting your income from them. In addition, some issue monthly or quarterly publications such as The George Putnam Fund's

Prudent Investor, in which financial advice is mixed with news about the Fund, its policies, and its dividends.

Furthermore, a shareholder is welcome at any time to visit the head office of his fund and watch its management at work, or discuss with its officials any questions he may have.

Fourth, owning securities through a mutual fund makes for a high degree of convenience. Should an individual investor own 100 different stocks, he would probably have 400 dividend checks to cash or deposit. In a fund he receives his share of the income, less operating expense. And, no matter how small his number of shares in the fund, he owns an interest in all the securities it holds.

Fifth, he is employing 24-hour-a-day professional management for his money. This management will select the securities he owns, spread his investments among enough companies to give him a cross section of industry, and take care to replace such issues as may have become overvalued or for which the future no longer seems bright. Being human, fund managers do not always make these changes as promptly as might be wished.

Sixth, should the investor's mutual fund shares become part of his estate because of his death, he has passed along to his widow or his heirs professional management which will relieve them of investment problems.

Despite all these advantages, there are some people who should not buy shares in mutual funds. No person whose life savings amount to only a few hundred dollars should have his nest egg anywhere but in a savings bank. The "thrill buyer" who haunts brokerage offices in his lunch hour, and who is always first on the street for closing quotations in the papers, and who buys prices rather than values, will find nothing in fund shares to attract him. Nor will the part-time professional speculator, always articulate about "the big one that got away." If he wants something he can pick up in March around 40, and which will be above 80 before Labor Day, he should buy a thermometer.

Policemen's Ball nothing!—I want to ask you about MUTUAL FUNDS.

What can be expected of mutual funds by those who do buy their shares? No miracles, to be sure. There is no widely distributed dream fund which will always be in cash during market declines, and in fast-moving stocks when securities are on their way to new highs. Nothing is perfect, some philosopher has remarked, except bachelors' wives and old maids' children.

Do not expect the impossible from your mutual fund. The investor looking for 10% usually gets it—in a final division of the assets. Your mutual fund will not rise in price when securities are declining, nor will it increase its payments to you when dividends in general are being reduced.

When the present head of one of the country's top-ranking investment management companies took office he said, "I promise you two things. I will be honest, and I will make mistakes." That is the spirit in which fund management approaches its job. You will get few miracles, but you will get a thoroughly workmanlike effort to accomplish the objectives of your fund, whatever type it may be.

At the National Mutual Fund Convention in Boston in 1953, during a panel meeting at which representatives of the press queried fund executives, this question was asked: "Does a decline in the securities markets mean that you face a difficult public relations job?" An answer which brought applause from the audience was: "No. If the investor understands what he owns, after a declining market his feeling will be 'Yes, my shares are lower in price, but I know that the management of my fund, with the same amount of money over the same period of time, has done a great deal better job for me than I could have done for myself.' "

So, unless you are a "market expert" (one who can tell you before 10 A.M. which stocks will go up, and after 3:30 P.M. can tell why they did not), let us step over together into the next chapter and see what the various types of mutual funds are like, and which may best suit your particular needs.

2. Which Fund for You?

Four main features of any investment—Which do you want most? —How bonds and stocks differ—What diversification is—What investment goal are you trying to reach?—Types of funds: balanced, stock, bond, and specialty funds—Prospectuses quoted—What closed-end investment companies are.

If you talked with someone familiar with securities, he would probably tell you that most people look for four things in an investment program. Most investments have these things in varying degrees—some more of one, some more of the others:

Safety, or security

Income

Appreciation (or market gain)

Marketability

The first letters of these four main elements of an investment program spell the word SIAM. That is easy to remember if you recall the riddle "What is the world's champion kibitzer?" to which the answer is "An unmarried Siamese twin."

No mutual fund (or any other investment you can make) can give you all four of these elements. An investment that came even close would be rare as a confession-story magazine cover showing a beautiful young woman with all her clothes on.

Usually people think of safety or security in an investment program in terms of savings banks, or bonds. It would be natural for them to look to mutual funds for the growth or risk portions of their programs, although there are funds which hold only investment-quality bonds.

So, as a person who may have money to invest, your first thought should be as to which one, or two, of these things you want most. As we will be looking at funds that hold only stocks, and only bonds, and others which hold combinations of the two, let us illustrate the difference by considering a predicament of our old friend the village blacksmith. Suppose the smith has been doing a nice business, shoeing horses, mending cracked whiffletrees, and so on, and he decides that with new and better equipment he could do more business and make more money.

He goes to the local banker, and after the usual comments on the weather and the sad state of the country have been exchanged he says "Fred, I was thinkin' of makin' the shop a little bigger, maybe. Might need some money. If I did, what would you say to takin' a mortgage?"

"Ike," says the banker. "I'll lend you money—sure, but not on a mortgage. Suppose I did take a mortgage on the smithy? All I'd get would be a certain fixed number of dollars now and then. Why don't I go partners with you? Then, the more you make with your new equipment, the more I'd make, too."

In effect, the banker is buying stock in the smithy. Instead of being a creditor, as a mortgage holder or a bondholder would be, he is a partner. If the business suffers, so will he, but the more money it makes, the more his share will be worth. For many purposes, bonds are splendid investments, but it will help you decide what type of fund you want if you keep in mind the difference between creditorship (bonds) and ownership (stocks).

Any fund you buy will give you three built-in things:
Selection (choosing the securities owned)
Diversification (spreading of risk)
Supervision (watching the securities owned)
Selection explains itself. Supervision we will talk about later

when we watch investment management at work. Diversification, or the spreading of risk, is easy to understand if we make a couple of mental pictures.

"I thank my fortune for it," says Antonio in Act I of Shakespeare's "Merchant of Venice" after hearing about a shipwreck which had lost a fortune for one of his friends who sent out all his worldly goods in a single ship, "my ventures are not in one bottom trusted." Chinese merchants had the same ideas hundreds of years before Shakespeare when they divided their cargoes and each took, in his own ship, one-twentieth of his own cargo and a like percentage of those of nineteen friends. If one prospered, all prospered. If one ship was sunk, the proportionate loss to each man was small.

To a farmer, diversification might mean crop rotation, or for a better example we might have him diversify by owning a wheat farm in the west, a cattle ranch in Texas, corn stands in Indiana, potato fields on Long Island, cotton plantations in the south, dairy herds in New Jersey, and breeding farms for sheep and hogs in still other parts of the country. His interests would be highly diversified.

Or a chicken raiser might diversify by purchasing 1000 baby chicks, knowing from his experience with the law of averages that even if a few died most of them would grow up to be good salable layers, or table poultry. If he used the same amount of money to buy one bird for show purposes, he would be speculating on the future of that single fowl.

A mutual fund gives you spreading of risk in many ways. It invests for you in many different businesses in many parts of the country and subject to many different sets of conditions. It puts your money to work in a much wider variety of ways than anyone but an extremely wealthy person could afford to do. And when it has put your eggs into all these baskets, it makes a day-by-day, year-in-and-year-out job of watching the baskets for you. When you consider owning shares in a mutual fund, remember you need not be a millionaire to invest like one.

Before we leave our three friends Selection, Diversification, and Supervision for a while, let us see what an entirely unbiased source has to say about them and their value to people who are looking for a medium of investment which may meet their needs. As you know, the Better Business Bureaus in various cities are constantly on the watch to protect their citizens, including investors. These Bureaus have issued through their National Association a series of booklets dealing with such topics as *Buying a Home, Advice on Legal Problems, Life Insurance, Saving Money,* and many others. Any of these booklets can be had for ten cents from your local Bureau, and among them is one entitled *FACTS You Should Know About Investment Companies.* On page 4 it says:

An investment company that is properly and honestly managed, offers a convenient and desirable medium of investment to all types of investors including trustees, institutions, etc., and particularly to those of limited financial means. There are several advantages in buying the securities of such a company. One important advantage is the factor of greater safety made available through diversification of the portfolio securities. Ordinarily, it would be impossible or impractical for small investors to endeavor to obtain such diversification for themselves.

The privilege of pooling convenient sums of money in a large fund managed by experienced men and thereby eliminating many investment problems of his own, is another advantage the well-managed investment company offers to the investor. Many such companies have elaborate facilities for research, statistical data and analyses of market trends which enable them to maintain a constant and intelligent supervision of their portfolios, whereas the average investor, whether or not he is familiar with the business of investing in individual securities, usually does not have the time and facilities to perform the many supervisory tasks which are so necessary to successful investing.

When you sit down with your investment dealer in his office, or in your own home, if he is going to do a good job in helping you select the fund you should have, his first step will be to do what he would probably call "determining your objective." This just means finding out what you want most in terms of risk you can afford: income, a chance that your money will grow, marketability, or the assurance that when you need the dollars represented by your shares you will be able to get them. This last is taken care of for you by the redemption feature common to all mutual funds, which gives you the right to present your shares for repurchase by the fund, at a price which may be lower or higher than you paid, on any business day.

As to the other three things you might want in your investment, your dealer will help you select a fund designed to furnish them in their order of importance as it appears to you. He knows the characteristics of the various funds, and will not advise you to buy a horse if you want milk, a canary to pull your plough, or a cow to sing beautiful songs to you.

So, he will talk about your objectives, which may include sending your child to college many years hence, accumulating enough money to go to Europe some day or for your husband to start his own business, or for you to retire when it is time to stop working. Or, you may simply want to amass what seems like a large enough sum of money to make you feel less timid about the future.

When you ask your dealer what kinds of funds there are, he will probably start with these: stock funds, bond funds, balanced funds (which hold both stocks and bonds), growth stock funds, and specialty funds. To get at the thinking behind each of these types, let us see what some representative prospectuses say about them. A *prospectus* is the booklet a dealer must give you when he offers you shares. It contains information you should have before deciding whether or not you want to invest.

A *stock fund* requires less explanation than some of the other types. It invests in common stocks, usually owning a broad list in which you have an interest in all the items, even though your dollar investment be small. Some of them center their attention upon market gains, others try for generous income. Here is a statement from the prospectus of Investment Company of America:

Ordinarily the assets of the Company consist principally of a diversified group of common stocks, but other types of securities may be held when deemed advisable. In the selection of securities, the possibilities of appreciation and potential dividends are given more weight than current dividend yield.

Bond Funds are what the name implies. Some hold only one type of bonds, perhaps the highest grade. Others hold bonds of junior grades. Investors who "don't like to own stocks," often find that ownership of bonds through a mutual fund is a handy way to own the senior securities without the inconvenience of coupon clipping and depositing. Here is a description, from its prospectus, of Manhattan Bond Fund:

The primary objective . . . is to obtain for shareholders a regular income derived from interest payments on a broadly diversified and continuously supervised group of bond investments. . . . Assets of the Fund are presently invested in selected bonds believed to be of good quality, but of less than first investment grade. An investment in many issues of such bonds is believed to involve substantially less risk to income and principal than ownership of a single bond of the same quality.

Balanced funds hold both bonds and stocks, and often preferred stocks as well. Most balanced funds keep a middle-of-the-road course in investing. They do not at any time put all your money into any one kind of securities, no matter how good the managements believe they are. Such funds are designed to afford the shareholder (1) the protection of good-grade bonds, (2) fairly generous income from preferred stocks, and (3) the chance for his money to grow, which is the basic quality for which common stocks are ordinarily bought.

True, the percentages of these securities will be changed from time to time, but that is just one more example of the value of the management the shareholder gets for his money. Changing the percentages should give a high degree of defense when things look bad or doubtful, and a higher degree of chance for profit when the business skies clear.

Balanced funds are not all alike. Their objectives differ, just as do those of investors. Here are quotations from the prospectuses of four such funds:

Eaton & Howard Balanced Fund:

Seeks as high and as dependable an income as may be obtained from a prudently managed investment account. It also seeks reasonable growth of both principal and income. The affairs of the Fund are conducted as the management would consider desirable if the Fund were an individual's portfolio and represented his entire investment program.

Axe-Houghton Fund B:

Objective is to produce reasonable income, long-term capital appreciation and safety of principal. The Fund's assets are invested in cash and government securities, bonds, preferred stocks, and common stocks, in such proportions and of such quality as are deemed best adapted to the current economic outlook. However, it is the policy not to invest more than 60% of its gross assets at cost in common stocks.

The George Putnam Fund:

Provides the investor with a balanced investment program under the active supervision of a full-time management organization. It is designed to serve those men and women who desire to make haste slowly in the investment of their savings rather than those individuals who seek big speculative gains.

Wellington Fund:

Is designed to provide the experienced professional investment management your money needs. In Wellington your dollars are invested in over 250 separate securities in many different industries and balanced among different types of securities—bonds, preferred and common stocks—thus reducing the risks of market fluctuation.

Next on the list of funds your dealer mentioned came those which invest in *growth stocks*. In the prospectus of Massachusetts Investors Growth Stock Fund they are defined as

. . . companies which possess better than ordinary potentialities for growth over a period of years. Generally speaking, such potentialities are indicated for companies which produce types of goods or services having relatively favorable long-term prospects for increasing demand, or which aggressively pursue policies of developing new and improved products or services and new and expanding markets through intensive research and resourceful management.

National Investors, which adopted its growth stock policy in 1939 and is believed to be the first fund to do so, in its prospectus says that such stocks are

those of companies believed able, over a period of years, subject to interim interruptions, to increase their sales and earnings at a greater rate than American business as a whole. Growth of a company may result from a number of factors—aggressive research for new products, new markets for old products, sound expansion of plant and equipment—but management ability most often is of paramount importance.

Next on the list came *specialty funds*. These usually confine their investments to a single industry. Typical are the following:

Television-Electronics Fund, founded on a belief in the present soundness and future growth prospects of the field of television, electronics, and radio.

Century Shares Trust, which invests in the shares of domestic and foreign insurance companies, banks and trust companies, and their subsidiaries.

Chemical Fund, the cornerstone of whose policy is reliance on the long-term growth of the chemical field.

Gas Industries Fund invests in

all types of securities identified with the gas industry, i.e., companies directly or indirectly engaged in whole or in part in the production, transmission or distribution of gas.

In addition to the above, there are portfolios within the larger structure of parent funds which offer single-industry investments. Typical of these are Group Securities, and Managed Funds, both of which have various single-industry packages such as automobile, electrical equipment, or steel shares.

In 1953 two new types of funds made their appearance. One was Atomic Development Mutual Fund, to invest in that field. The other was Capital Venture Fund, which states in its prospectus that it is intended as a vehicle for investors who cannot make adequate provision for the future out of after-tax income, do not require additional current income from their investments, and are in a position to assume the risk of investment in the more speculative equity securities.

One other type of fund is the series known as Keystone Custodian Funds. They differ from others in that their portfolios are based on the theory of the indestructibility of class, and each contains securities of only one quality and type: for example, high-grade bonds, high-income preferred stocks, or volatile common stocks.

If you are well along in years, you will probably want a fund geared to pay fairly generous income. If you have recently started business, and are earning enough to put something aside with the expectation of being able to do so for many years, your choice might be a common stock or growth stock fund. If you are somewhere in between, your best use of funds may be a selection of several for various purposes.

As a matter of fact, almost any fund run by capable people should do a good job for you in the long run. An old Negro loaded his wagon with wheat to drive to the mill. One neighbor advised him to go by the county highway, another suggested he go down by the river, and a third swore his best route was the

tory as of January 1, 1958, there were 15 mutual funds offering shares at no acquisition cost. They accounted for less than 2.3% of the total assets of the 177 mutual funds in the United States, and had less than 1% of the shareholders.

In June 1953 Governor Fine of Pennsylvania signed the Snowden Bill, making certain mutual funds legal for trust investments for amounts up to one-third of a trust account. Here were the qualifications set forth by the Bill for such use:

1. Fund must be registered under the Investment Company Act of 1940.

2. It must have assets of at least $10 million on date of purchase by the trustee.

3. It must have no senior capitalization or bank loans with priority ahead of the fund's stock.

4. It must have paid dividends in twelve out of the past sixteen years.

Of the fifteen no-acquisition-cost mutual funds listed in the *Directory*, only three met these requirements.

Why, one may well ask, does an organization which cannot profit by the distribution of shares sponsor a mutual fund? There are two reasons. One is that if people buy enough shares, the management fee will in time become worth while in size. Such funds are operated by people who do investment advisory work. They are not primarily in the mutual fund business. Another reason you will see in the following description, sent in for the *Mutual Fund Directory* by the managers of Dodge & Cox Fund:

The Fund is maintained primarily to extend the services of the firm of Dodge & Cox, investment managers, to clients whose funds are insufficient in size to permit economical administration as separate accounts.

These *convenience accounts* come about in this way. A wealthy client is pleased with the job a firm has done for him, and wants them to manage, on the same percentage fee he pays for his large account, small amounts belonging to members of his family, his favorite nieces, or perhaps even some of his business friends. The investment counsel firm simply cannot afford to do so. There is just as much work to managing an account with $20,000 in assets as one ten times as large. More work, in fact, for the problem of diversification is much harder with small amounts. So, when this happens too many times, either business is lost by the firm, or a new mutual fund is born.

Your dealer will give you all necessary facts before you decide what fund or funds will be best for you. As background for what professional securities supervisors do with your money when it is entrusted to them, let us see in the next chapter some of the changes they have made in their portfolio holdings in recent years, and some of the reasons why it is hard even for them, no matter what business and economic conditions may be, to pick the right stock.

3. What Is Management Worth?

Choosing your management—Do you know what to buy and sell, and when?—Can you do so ahead of the crowd?—The Favorite Fifty stocks most widely held by investment companies and how they have changed—How investment opportunities in industries change—What the Dow Industrial Average is—"Many that are last shall be first"—How investment information is gathered.

Every weekday at 10:15 a group of men sit down around a table on the 21st floor of 65 Broadway in New York City and face what sounds like a staggering task. They are responsible for the intelligent investment of over $465,000,000 of other people's money.

The above is the opening paragraph of a booklet describing the work of Union Service Corporation. Later on, the text reads:

When a person buys shares in an investment company he makes an important decision. He entrusts the management of his money to other people—usually people he doesn't know. He says, in effect, "Here is my money. You take it and invest it for me as wisely as you can."

His decision may be a good or poor one. He may have made it with great care, studying the past records of a number of investment companies before turning his money over to any of them. But whether it is good or bad only time will tell. The answer depends to a considerable extent on the ability and experience of the people who are to manage the investment of his funds and on what these people have to work with—the breadth and depth of the organization behind them.

This makes sense. In this chapter we will look at some management thinking and what came of it. Also we shall review a few of the decisions such management has made, and see why.

First, let us knock down one straw man which seems to bother a lot of people. This is the idea that an investor can beat the game by reading the reports of investment companies, and following their purchases or sales by doing the same thing himself with one or two of the securities they have bought or sold.

This point comes up from time to time at the annual Mutual Fund Conventions, and at one such meeting it was covered by Charles F. Eaton, Jr., head of Eaton & Howard, Inc., of Boston. In stressing the fact that isolated transactions may not in themselves be important to the management picture as a whole, and that they are in no way a guide to what the individual investor should do, he said:

The big point on this is more basic. The mutual fund is offering diversification and management. The fact that you have selected a new baby to go into the portfolio doesn't mean that you have shot the old baby. The idea that a new stock is what you think is the best thing in the market is ridiculous. It is the family, not the baby, that we are selling. Emphasis on any one item is dangerous and could be misleading.

In other words, an investment fund management has an overall plan (its objective) to which all its purchases and sales must be related. The fund, and the investor, may have such separate goals that action by the fund may be in no way helpful to the individual.

That points up a definite advantage in owning your securities through a mutual fund. Changes in the holdings are made for you, automatically. You need not consider related facts about the stock you are thinking of buying or selling, make your decision, then go to your safe-deposit box and get out the old stock, take it to your broker, sell it, buy the other issue, wait for it to be transferred to your name, and then put the new certificate in your box.

Furthermore, if too many investors get the same idea at the same time (and it makes no difference whether they want to buy or sell) they might easily spoil the market for each other. If they all wanted to buy, they would force the price up beyond a reasonable figure. If they wanted to sell, they would depress the price. This is particularly true when the investor is taking advice from a service which sends him bulletins or letters telling him what to do. If 5000 investors received a Buy or Sell recommendation the same morning, and most of them decided to act on it, you can imagine the result.

As illustrations of what some of the fund managements have been thinking and doing in the past few years, let us look at some actual cases. First, you will see in Table 1 the list known as the Favorite Fifty. This is an analysis showing, by dollar value, the listed stocks most popular with professional management. It is copyrighted by Vickers Associates, Inc., and is a part of the service they supply known as their *Guide to Investment Trust Portfolios.*

The Favorite Fifty list is published twice a year. Table 1 shows the stocks owned on June 30, 1957, with the number of investment companies holding each, and the dollar value in millions of the shares so held. Holders included 60 closed-end trusts and over 165 mutual funds, with investable assets of about $14 billion. Stocks owned by less than 15 companies or funds, and individual blocks of stock held for control or what appears to be a similar purpose, were omitted. The market value of the Favorite Fifty as shown was about $3.5 billion, and represented about 25% of the total assets of the open and closed-end companies studied.

TABLE 1. FAVORITE FIFTY[a]

Funds Holding		Dollar Value
110	Standard Oil Company (New Jersey)	187.7
62	International Business Machines Corp.	142.4
47	Amerada Petroleum Corporation	138.5
82	United States Steel Corporation	126.1
67	Bethlehem Steel Corporation	125.8
75	The Texas Company	124.8
68	Gulf Oil Corporation	118.6
62	Standard Oil Company of California	107.6
67	Aluminium, Ltd.	104.5
59	Continental Oil Company	101.8
66	Goodyear Tire & Rubber Company	95.2
59	International Paper Company	93.1
73	duPont (E. I.) de Nemours & Company	87.9
85	General Electric Company	87.2
79	General Motors Corporation	85.9
79	Socony Mobil Oil Company	82.2
43	National Lead Company	81.9
46	Shell Oil Company	71.2
54	Armco Steel Corporation	67.0
48	Goodrich (B. F.) Company	65.9
72	Union Carbide & Carbon Corporation	63.3
16	The Superior Oil Company, (California)	62.3
72	Phillips Petroleum Company	60.0
29	Firestone Tire & Rubber Company	58.4
50	Sinclair Oil Corporation	57.8
53	Republic Steel Corporation	57.8
49	Aluminum Company of America	53.3
46	Standard Oil Company (Indiana)	51.6
29	Louisiana Land & Exploration	51.1
64	Kennecott Copper Corporation	50.5

Table 1—*Continued*

Funds Holding		Dollar Value
36	Minnesota Mining & Manufacturing Co.	48.4
53	International Nickel Co. of Canada, Ltd.	47.7
60	American Telephone & Telegraph Co.	47.1
38	Cities Service Company	45.2
24	Reynolds Metals Company	44.4
33	Southern Railway Company	43.2
51	Central & South West Corporation	41.3
52	General Public Utilities Corporation	41.0
45	Texas Utilities Company	40.9
29	United States Gypsum Company	39.8
33	Youngstown Sheet & Tube Co.	39.8
37	Phelps Dodge Corporation	39.1
35	Pfizer, (Chas.) & Co., Inc.	38.7
51	Monsanto Chemical Company	37.7
48	Westinghouse Electric Corporation	37.6
43	Southern Company (The)	36.8
51	Atchison, Topeka & Santa Fe Railway Co.	36.4
32	Minneapolis-Honeywell Regulator Co.	34.6
35	Halliburton Oil Well Cementing Co. (Del.)	34.2
45	Middle South Utilities, Inc.	33.9

ᵃ Reprinted with the permission of Vickers Associates, Inc.

Here is a list (you can compare it with Table 1) of the top ten stocks in the June 30, 1953 Favorite Fifty:

Amerada Petroleum	General Electric
Standard Oil (N.J.)	Goodrich Company
Continental Oil	Texas Company
International Paper	Standard Oil (Cal.)
E. I. duPont	Gulf Oil Corporation

In the four years elapsed between the two lists, 17 stocks dropped from the 1953 roster and 17 were added. During the period, downward changes in rating saw Westinghouse Electric go from 12th to 45th; Kennecott Copper from 14th to 30th and Atchison, Topeka & Santa Fe Railway from 15th to 47th. On the up side, Goodyear Tire & Rubber Co. moved from 45th place to 11th; Bethlehem Steel from 29th to 4th and International Business Machines from 27th to 2nd place. These changes are shown purely as illustrations, and should not be taken as indicating opinions as to future values.

Table 1 gives an over-all picture of fairly recent investment company portfolio management. To be more specific, let us look at a mutual fund and see what it did. Here is Table 2, showing the portfolio by industries of Affiliated Fund at the end (October 31) of five of its fiscal years.

TABLE 2.   DIVERSIFICATION OF ASSETS

Stocks	Percentage of Assets October 31				
	1953	1952	1951	1950	1949
Agricultural equipment	0.2	0.5	1.3	1.9	2.8
Aircraft	0.8	0.7	0.9	1.4	1.9
Automotive	0.1	0.2	0.4	0.7	6.3
Banking	9.3	9.3	4.5	—	—
Building	1.7	1.1	1.2	2.3	5.1
Chemical	0.9	1.1	3.2	5.6	9.5
Coal	0.1	0.2	0.4	0.8	0.8
Container	3.4	3.8	4.0	1.9	1.6
Drug	3.4	3.2	3.5	0.1	0.8
Electrical equipment	0.5	0.3	0.4	—	2.1
Electric light and power	22.0	23.0	17.9	16.0	6.6
Finance	—	—	—	—	2.3
Food	8.5	7.2	5.0	0.4	2.0
Gold	1.1	1.1	1.3	1.6	0.8
Machinery	0.4	0.2	—	0.6	0.8
Motion picture	2.1	.1.8	3.3	2.6	1.5

TABLE 2. DIVERSIFICATION OF ASSETS—Continued

	Percentage of Assets October 31				
Stocks	1953	1952	1951	1950	1949
Natural gas	12.1	8.5	6.6	4.6	4.2
Nonferrous metal	1.0	1.3	1.5	3.6	4.6
Office equipment	2.0	1.9	2.3	2.0	2.2
Oil	4.5	7.3	14.0	29.9	19.1
Oil service and supply	0.5	0.3	0.5	0.4	0.3
Radio and television	0.6	0.6	0.3	—	—
Railroad	3.6	4.7	4.5	5.2	4.8
Railroad equipment	0.9	0.8	0.7	1.0	1.1
Rubber	—	—	—	0.1	1.1
Shoe	0.1	—	—	—	—
Steel and refractory	—	—	—	0.4	3.1
Store—department	2.5	3.1	4.1	4.1	3.2
Store—grocery	2.1	1.6	1.9	2.3	0.6
Store—variety	3.6	3.5	2.8	0.4	0.8
Telephone	1.4	2.1	3.0	—	—
Textile	0.6	0.9	1.6	2.4	2.5
Tobacco	7.6	7.3	4.2	5.5	5.8
Total stocks	97.6	97.6	95.3	97.8	98.3
Cash and Receivables, Net	2.4	2.4	4.7	2.2	1.7
Total	100.0	100.0	100.0	100.0	100.0

You will see from Table 2 that over the 4-year period shown there were sizable increases in stocks representing banking and natural gas, as well as electric light and power. Also there were decreases in holdings of oil stocks and chemicals.

Whether you are an investor making his own decisions, or a mutual fund management with many sources of information, you must not only select the proper securities but you must be able to do so, if maximum results are to be obtained, before others realize their possibilities. In this connection, the increase in holdings of electric light and power stocks shown in Table 2 is of special interest. During the four years, the managers of Affiliated Fund believed they saw neglected opportunities in this field. From a 6.6% holding in such stocks, their percentage was increased to 23% in 1952. This decision was made because studies showed that such stocks, based on the management's estimates of their future earnings and dividends, could be bought substantially under their real values.

The decrease in percentage of oil stocks held presents an interesting story. As of October 31, 1948 such holdings accounted for less than 10% of assets of the Fund. In 1949 and 1950 there was much pessimistic talk about overproduction in the oil industry, and growing foreign competition. Believing that value was more important than price, and foreseeing better than average market results, substantial purchases were made. By the end of 1950 oil stocks were definitely in fashion, and their market prices, the Affiliated management felt, reflected overoptimism. As you see by Table 2, percentage of such holdings was materially reduced.

One more comment is of interest in connection with the thinking behind the percentages changes in Table 2. At the end of 1949, automobile stocks were still in favor, and Affiliated Fund held a large block of General Motors. However, the management believed greater opportunities existed in other industries. The General Motors holding was sold and the money reinvested in Socony-Vacuum Oil. General Motors shares continued their market rise, advancing another ten points, but the Socony-Vacuum holding (about twice as many shares as the General Motors which was sold) in its market performance far more than repaid the management for the exchange.

When it was felt that the Socony-Vacuum shares reflected their full market value, they in turn were sold, and the money reinvested in Texas Utilities, still in the Affiliated portfolio on October 31, 1953.

This illustration is given, not to praise any individual fund management, but to point out that under such management no purchase made is considered a "till death do us part" situation. Investment values are always relative. Any holding, in the eyes of professional management, is regarded in two ways. First of these is its *market* potential (this means how much can be expected of it in the way of market profit, or income) if held in the portfolio. The second is its *cash* potential. This means that if the fund had cash in hand, instead of the number of shares of stock represented by the holding being considered, would the particular holding be purchased at that time, or would the money be better employed buying something else.

In connection with changes made in holdings, an interesting situation developed in the late fall of 1953. Tobacco stocks, long highly regarded as investment issues and held in many investment portfolios for market stability as well as income, began to suffer from overindulgence in gadgets and sales gimmicks. New kinds of tips, various sorts of filters, king-size cigarettes, all brought new merchandising and sales problems. The business had become more competitive, and it appeared that profit margins of the tobacco companies might be impaired. On top of all this came the sudden impact of the lung cancer scare and its bad publicity.

Because of the competitive situation, Wellington Fund in the few months before October 1953 had reduced its tobacco stock holdings from a market value of some $4,800,000 to less than $600,000. When the lung cancer scare hit, and its effect on the cigarette stocks had made itself felt, Selected American Shares (which owned 3000 American Tobacco and 8000 Lorillard as of September 30) took the opportunity to buy at the reduced prices an additional 4000 Lorillard and 3000 shares of Liggett & Myers.

Here are two fund managements with one (Wellington) taking defensive action and the other (Selected) taking offensive action. One sold a major part of an industry holding because it looked for lower prices. When the unfavorable publicity (which had not come out at the time of the Wellington move) had had its day in the public eye and ear, the other fund went bargain hunting.

On this point of bargain hunting, it might be well to add an additional thought. Mutual funds always have (or can find through the sale of less desirable holdings) cash to take advantage of such situations. This illustrates the cash potential aspect of fund management about which you read earlier in this chapter.

Before we go further in discussing management, let us get acquainted with an index by which many people like to judge market performance. This index is what is called the "Dow"— its full title being the Dow-Jones Industrial Average. It is owned and published by *The Wall Street Journal*, which sends the changes in the average over its wire system several times a day.

Should you walk into a broker's office, or the office of an investment dealer in any city you care to name, and ask the first person you saw "How's the market?," chances are he would say "Up a point," or "Off a half," meaning that the figure representing the thirty investment stocks in the Dow Average had gone up or off by that amount.

The "Dow" dates back well before the turn of this century. It is by all odds the best-known market index. It will not tell you what the market is going to do, but is helpful in gauging stock movements in the past.

This index is introduced here both because of the wide general interest it commands and because it contains many high-grade "blue chip" stocks which traders and investors follow as a matter of general market interest. You will see in Table 3 what the stocks are:

TABLE 3.   YEAR BY YEAR CHANGES IN RELATIVE STANDING OF THE THIRTY
STOCKS COMPRISING THE DOW-JONES INDUSTRIAL AVERAGES[a]

	1948	1949	1950	1951	1952	1953	1954	1955	1956	1957
Allied Chemical	17	15	19	6	22	17	18	17	27	23
American Can	8	3	29	8	3	5	28	21	26	10
Am. Smelting	16	25	10	5	28	29	8	19	8	30
Am. Tel. & Tel.	10	27	22	22	21	15	29	22	21	11
Am. Tobacco	25	9	30	27	18	18	30	11	25	7
Bethlehem Steel	19	26	3	20	13	22	1	2	6	25
Chrysler	29	6	23	24	1	30	24	14	29	22
Corn Products	21	8	25	23	24	7	27	24	15	2
duPont	11	1	7	16	17	4	11	8	28	13
Eastman Kodak	13	21	20	25	25	8	13	18	11	1
General Electric	5	19	17	9	5	2	9	12	16	9
General Foods	3	11	26	26	8	3	22	13	22	3
General Motors	9	10	11	13	2	25	7	3	20	21
Goodyear	15	22	4	4	4	14	2	15	2	8
Int. Harvester	23	23	18	17	27	26	19	26	13	27
Int. Nickel	2	29	12	10	11	28	4	5	1	29
Johns-Manville	18	5	24	2	12	24	20	25	9	20
Loew's-Int. Paper	30	12	27	15	29	12	6	29	23	16
Nat'l Distillers	27	7	15	7	30	27	21	28	5	19
National Steel	4	24	1	21	26	21	17	20	10	28
Procter & Gamble	20	2	13	30	23	11	16	23	17	4
Sears Roebuck	7	17	16	19	14	10	23	6	30	14
St'd. Oil of Cal.	6	28	5	14	9	23	15	16	12	12
St'd. Oil of N. J.	22	30	6	1	20	20	12	7	7	15
Texas Company	26	16	8	3	19	13	14	4	18	6
Union Carbide	1	18	14	12	10	9	26	10	14	18
United Aircraft	12	14	9	18	6	1	5	9	4	24
U. S. Steel	24	13	2	29	15	19	3	1	3	26
Westinghouse Electric	28	4	21	11	7	6	10	30	19	5
Woolworth	14	20	28	28	16	16	25	27	24	17

[a] This table is published through the courtesy of Keystone Custodian Funds.
It was first used in their bulletin *Keynotes* in January, 1948. Adjustment has
been made for all stock splits or stock dividends of 10% or more. Loew's was
replaced by International Paper July 3, 1956.

Probably when you have been talking about investments some time, you have heard someone make a remark like this: "I don't know why you need professional management. Why not just buy the ones that did best last year? Stocks like that certainly must be all right."

If you feel that this statement is correct, devote a little time to the study of Table 3. In the first three gospels of the New Testament there appears four times the statement that many that are first shall be last, and the last shall be first.* While of course the speaker had no reference to common stocks, the point is obvious.

From a quick review of this record, you will see that more than half the time the leading stock dropped to the lower half of the list the following year. Only one of the top 10 in the 1956 standing remained in that group in 1957. International Nickel, first in 1956, dropped to 29th the following year. No stock has headed the list in two consecutive years. Only one to be in first place twice has been Chrysler. After leading in 1947 it was 29th in 1948. First again in 1952, it was last in 1953.

Changes upward can be surprising, too. Eastman Kodak, which led in 1957, came up from 11th place to do so after being better than 13th only once in the preceding 8 years. National Steel rose to first in 1950 after being 24th. So did Chrysler in 1952. Sears Roebuck once jumped from 29th to first. This brief review illustrates the difficulty of selecting the next "top performer."

What, then, will professional management do when faced with the various problems of selection and supervision on which we have touched lightly here? Some maintain their own organizations. Others add to their own staff work by employing outside talent. Chemical Fund, for instance, retains Arthur D. Little, Inc., one of the foremost chemical consulting firms. John P. Chase, Inc. of Boston, an investment management

* Matthew 19:30 and 20:16. Mark 10:31. Luke 13:30.

It doesn't help the securities, but it keeps you from losing sleep
over them.

firm with over $300,000,000 in the accounts of individuals and institutions, is employed by sponsors of both Shareholders Trust of Boston and of Electronics Investment Corporation.

Value Line Fund and the more recently formed Value Line Income Fund, together with Value Line Special Situations Fund—the three having assets of some $90,000,000—are supervised by Arnold Bernhard & Co., Inc., publishers of *The Value Line Investment Survey*.

We spoke a few pages back about offensive and defensive changes as an aid to management results. Besides changes made in actual portfolio holdings, varying the amounts of cash held can be helpful in obtaining the objectives of a fund. In 1929, Wellington Fund had reduced its common stocks holdings to 33% of its assets, the thinking of its management being that it just was not "in the wood" for stocks to be selling at 50 times earnings. In 1942, it was back up to 78% in common stocks. New England Fund, which features a highly flexible policy, has varied the defensive percentage of its portfolio. As of September 30, 1953 its common stock section accounted for 60% of assets, comparing with 53% on December 31, 1957. Previous year ends showed these percentages of common stock:

1943	92	1946	52	1950	61
1944	88	1947	68	1955	59
1945	67	1948	73	1956	56

When you talk with your investment dealer about the fund he is recommending to you, ask him about the management work connected with the supervision of its portfolio. If he cannot tell you, ask him to bring along the fund's wholesale man, or somebody from the management department, next time he calls.

If you do not want to go into the matter that deeply, you can probably get a good idea of the management from the literature of the fund. Such a booklet—the one quoted at the opening of this chapter—is available from Union Service Corp. Another, in somewhat less formal style, and offering a friendly invitation to see how a typical management department works, is *A Visit with National Management*, issued by National Securities & Research Corp. Other funds have booklets they will be glad to send you, or you can get them from your investment man. Many show pictures of their top men, and give thumbnail sketches of their business experience and other connections.

In the main, investment research work, on which the decisions of the various management committees are carried out, depends on facts compiled by fund statisticians from their various sources of information, plus additional material gathered by their analysts on field trips to corporations in whose securities they have, or may have, an interest.

This type of work Charles F. Eaton, Jr. described beautifully in a talk he gave his organization as it approached its 30th anniversary.

Statistics have their place . . . but they are largely a matter of past history. The analyst is much more than a statistician. He is well informed not only of what has gone on in the past but of what is happening now. He is aware of the plans, hopes, and fears of the managements involved. He absorbs knowledge so that his views of the future can be based upon intelligent reasoning.

We use such information . . . but we go further in building up personal contacts with managements of companies. We see them at their places of business as well as in our own office. We inspect their plants and properties. We invite their thoughts and comments in an endeavor to gain some insight into the progress and the future prospects of their companies. . . . We are helped in our judgment of a company by information which we get from its officers, from its competitors, and from its bankers.

Good contacts with leaders in industry and finance are a priceless asset to any investment management organization. It is an asset which it takes time to acquire, as it is based upon mutual confidence. No responsible corporation officer or banker will give you information to which you are not entitled, or information which he may feel is in danger of being misused. But he can help you acquire a basic knowledge and understanding of a corporation's affairs, without which the financial statements by themselves lose much of their significance.

No investment management is infallible, but from this brief survey of such work it should be evident that a full-time, professional investment management firm is better equipped than the individual investor to (1) get basic information on which to form opinions, (2) evaluate the information properly after it is in hand, and (3) act on it with a minimum of inconvenience and a maximum of dispatch.

These assurances, plus the convenience of owning many securities in a single certificate, are the basic reasons why it is worth while to invest through a mutual fund.

Since there are so many stock funds, and since even the balanced funds usually have a major proportion of their assets in stocks, it might be well to look at some of the experiences people have had in buying and holding lists of stocks selected not as choice investments, but as groups of stocks chosen as representative cross sections of American industry.

4. Ways to Invest in Stocks

Sure, you can lose money in stocks—What dollar cost averaging is, and what its investment advantages are—A 1929-1953 stock program and its results—What the University of Michigan found out about common stock investment—How Harvard handles its $500,-000,000 endowment fund—What some other colleges have done with their investment accounts.

The number of securities upon the market is very large. For a small investor to make an intelligent selection from these—indeed, to pass an intelligent judgment upon a single one—is ordinarily impossible. He lacks the ability, the facilities, the training, and the time essential to a proper investigation. Unless his purchase is to be little better than a gamble, he needs the advice of an expert, who, combining special knowledge with judgment, has the facilities and incentive to make a thorough investigation.

This quotation is from the book *Other People's Money*, written by the late Louis D. Brandeis, Associate Justice, Supreme Court of the United States.

Sure—you can lose money buying common stocks. You can buy a no-good dog, or you can buy an excellent stock at the wrong time. This chapter has nothing to do with speculation in stocks. It was Mark Twain who said "There are two times that no man should speculate—when he cannot afford it, and when he can."

Many stocks become worthless. Your investment dealer probably has on his shelves a huge volume entitled *Obsolete Securities*, to which he refers when someone comes in with a stock or bond for which no market can be readily found.

When prizes used to be given for material in *The Bawl Street Journal*, a humorous burlesque of *The Wall Street Journal* published once a year by The Bond Club of New York, one winner was a Letter to the Inquiring Investor Editor.

"I have enough worthless securities to paper a room," wrote this bewildered investor. "Can you tell me what to do?"

"Of course," answered the Inquiring Investor Editor. "Paper a room."

Here are a couple of actual experiences with stocks. First, part of a letter received by the late Carl C. Lamb, formerly West Coast manager for Waddell & Reed, Inc.

I was cleaning out my desk recently and found five stock certificates that my father had purchased many years ago. These certificates were beautifully engraved on a fine grade of bond paper and represented a total investment of $1,450. Now they do not make good wall paper. These stocks were purchased by my father at various times. He invested $200 in one company in November 1916; $600 in another March 1919; $200 in November 1919 in the same company; $350 in May and $100 in June 1932 in another company. At the time of his passing, they were worthless.

There is no doubt . . . when my father purchased these securities they were represented as offering marvelous opportunities for income and growth. In fact none of them *ever paid one cent in dividends*. I am sure my father considered them a good speculation. In the light of what happened, he could have fared much better in a crap game. . . .

"Yes," you may say, "but that fellow didn't know anything about stocks." Here is another example.

About 14 years ago there died one of the best-informed and most popular younger men in Wall Street. He had been in the investment business for many years, and was a partner in one of the leading stock exchange firms. His brother, who acted as executor of the estate, found in the safe-deposit box worthless securities once with a value of more than $30,000. They had been bought from time to time as good speculations.

The brother, then a top executive of one of the country's leading mutual fund sponsor firms, kept the certificates in his desk, showing them as dramatic proof of the need of careful selection of securities, plus careful watching after they have been bought.

We are now going to look at a way of buying stocks officially called *dollar cost averaging*. Do not be alarmed by the high-sounding name. All it means is this. You buy securities by continuing to purchase the same one, and putting in the *same number of dollars* each time at regular intervals, instead of buying the same number of *shares*.

You could do the same thing with apples. Suppose you went to your favorite fruit stand and said to the owner "Joe, let me have one of your best apples."

"Fine," says Joe. "Very nice apple today. Him ten-a cent."

You pay your dime, take the apple and go your way. Three months later you come back and ask for the same. "Apple today very cheap," Joe tells you. "Two apple—ten-a cent." Three months later, in the dead of winter, you again approach the fruit stand. This time Joe shakes his head. "Big snow storm," says he. "Apple, he go way up. Good-a apple now, twenty cent each."

So, for the same amount of money each time, you would have invested first in one apple, then in two, and the third time in half an apple. You bought more when they were cheap, and less when they were high.

Here is the same sort of thing in figures:

This first example is *not* dollar cost averaging. You buy 100 shares of a stock at $10 each, 100 at $6 and 100 at $2 so you have 300 shares for $1,800 and your average price is $6 per share. If the price goes back to $6 you are even.

Here is how dollar cost averaging would use the same money:

$600 buys	60 shares at $10
$600 buys	100 shares at 6
$600 buys	300 shares at 2
	460

While the average of the three prices is still $6, your *average cost* is $3.913. If the stock goes back to $6 you are not just even—you have a profit of $960, or 53% on your investment.

Listen to Raymond Trigger, editor of *Investor Magazine*. He says:

Dollar Cost Averaging means simply this—you must be in a position to undertake the investment of a fixed number of dollars at regular periods . . . monthly, quarterly, or semi-annually. Then *do* it. No matter how pessimistic you may be . . . no matter how pessimistic everyone else may be . . . do not interrupt your plan. Select for your investment a security that is likely to fluctuate as the general market fluctuates.

To this comment one more point should be added. Be sure you invest in a security which will be there for your purpose as long as you want to continue your plan. Buying one which became worthless would of course defeat your purpose. So choose one that will be there.

In her book *Practical Formulas for Successful Investing*, investment authority Lucile Tomlinson states:

No one has yet discovered any other formula for investing which can be used with so much confidence of ultimate success, regardless of what may happen to security prices, as Dollar Cost Averaging.

There will be more comment about Miss Tomlinson and her book in our Recommended Reading section, and more about formula investing later on in these pages.

No reader should get the impression that dollar cost averaging will solve all investment problems for him. In fact, it is a requirement under rules administered by the National Association of Securities Dealers, Inc. that if a dealer offers you an investment plan based on this method he must tell you that:

1. There will be a loss if you discontinue your plan when the market value of your securities is less than their cost.

2. Securities will fluctuate, and this method involves continuous investment at regular intervals regardless of price levels.

3. You must take into account your financial ability to continue your plan through periods of low price levels.

4. Such plans do not and cannot protect against loss in value in declining markets.

With this introduction to dollar cost averaging in mind, let us take two excellent illustrations of how it has actually worked out on broad lists of stocks, not carefully chosen for any particular purpose, but representing fair cross sections of American industry.

Our first illustration is quoted from an advertisement which appeared in many newspapers in November 1953, inserted by a nationally known New York Stock Exchange firm. All the figures were computed by Standard & Poor's Corporation. Full allowance was made for all brokerage fees and federal income taxes for a married man with 2 children and an average annual salary of $8,000.

SO YOU'D LIKE TO RETIRE IN ABOUT 25 YEARS . . .

That's fine, we don't blame you. The only problem for most people is—will they be able to? Will they have enough income to enjoy the rest that they've earned?

We can't answer that question for you, of course.

But we do think that even a modest investment program—the regular purchase of sound common stocks over a period of years—can be a big part of that answer.

Why?

Because that's what the record shows. Suppose, for instance, that it was the year 1929—about as bad a time as you could pick—when you decided to start investing toward your retirement. You had enough insurance for protection, enough savings for emergencies, so you began to put $1,000 a year into common stocks.

Now we're not sure which stocks we would have suggested then, and we don't want to be accused of picking and choosing by hindsight, either.

So let's say, you bought $1,000 worth of a typical stock—a composite of 50 industrial stocks—the ones used to make up the well-known Standard & Poor's Index of daily stock prices.

Suppose that you had followed your program faithfully, and had bought $1,000 worth of that typical stock every year on July 1, starting in 1929. In 1953 you wanted to retire. Just where would you stand?

Well, let's look.

In the 24 years through June 30th of that year, you would have invested $24,000 all told, and you would have bought 934 shares of that typical stock.

At mid-year 1953, those 934 shares alone would have been worth $47,969 . . .

But you would have received another $24,192 in dividends over the years . . .

And you could have used those dividends to buy another 811 shares of your typical stock worth $41,656.

In other words, you could have retired on June 30th, 1953 with a grand total of 1,745 shares of typical stock with a market value of $89,625.

And if you continued to receive just a 5% return in dividends—the current average for 9 out of 10 stocks on the New York Stock Exchange was then 6.4%—you could count on an annual income of just about $4,500—without ever touching your principal at all!

But what if you had had to sell out somewhere along the line because you suddenly needed the cash? The answer is, that counting dividends, you could have sold out and shown a profit in any year after the first four.

Of course, this is the story of what has happened *since* 1929.

We can't promise that you'd benefit from the same kind of market movement over the next 20 or 25 years. It might be either more or less advantageous. Similarly we can't promise the same dividends, either.

But we do think on the basis of the record—a record established through good times and bad, through war and peace—that more people should consider what common stocks can contribute to their retirement.

What the results of this investment were, year by year, you can see in Table 4 which follows. Standard & Poor's presented this in the October 12, 1953 issue of its *Outlook*. In commenting on the process involved the text of the accompanying article said in part:

Dollar Cost Averaging has the advantage of being an unemotional approach that eliminates guesswork in attempting to pick market tops and bottoms.

The simple arithmetical principle involved is that the same amount of money will buy more shares when the price is low than when the price is high. As a consequence, the average *cost* of purchases will be lower than the average *price* no matter what the various prices may be, although this does not rule out the possibility of a paper loss at some intermediate phase. [Italics supplied.] Dollar Cost Averaging avoids the normal human impulse toward overoptimism when the market is up and excessive conservatism when it is down.

You will see from Table 4 that for the $25,000 the investor put in (which included a 1953 payment) plus reinvested dividends amounting to $28,429.87, the combined market value of the fund on June 30, 1953 was $91,902.89, compared with the total of $53,429.87 which had been put to work. This was a gain of $37,195.36 or 72%. If the investor had decided he would take his dividends in cash instead of reinvesting them, his $25,000 would on June 30, 1953 have been worth $50,084.78.

Our second illustration is from a study made by Professors Wilford J. Eiteman and Frank P. Smith, staff members at the School of Business Administration, University of Michigan. Commenting on the growing public interest in common stocks, these gentlemen introduce their study by saying:

TABLE 4. RESULTS OF 25 YEARS OF SYSTEMATIC INVESTING IN COMMON STOCKS
Based on 50 Stocks in Standard & Poor's Daily Industrial Index

	Investment			Cuml. Cost	Market Value (Dec. 31)		
	Primary	Reinvestment of Dividends	Total		Primary Fund	Reinvested Fund	Total
1929	$1,000.00	....	....	....	$713.95	....	....
1930	1,000.00	$14.42	$1,014.42	$2,014.42	1,311.42	$10.57	$1,321.99
1931	1,000.00	53.66	1,053.66	3,068.08	1,186.19	31.63	1,217.82
1932	1,000.00	86.90	1,086.90	4,154.98	2,477.90	101.82	2,579.72
1933	1,000.00	97.52	1,097.52	5,252.50	5,141.00	335.62	5,476.62
1934	1,000.00	143.73	1,143.73	6,396.23	6,158.53	475.51	6,634.04
1935	1,000.00	203.94	1,203.94	7,600.17	9,988.99	954.45	10,943.44
1936	1,000.00	298.83	1,298.83	8,899.00	13,827.75	1,586.05	15,413.80
1937	1,000.00	618.46	1,618.46	10,517.46	9,666.95	1,430.30	11,097.25
1938	1,000.00	824.04	1,824.04	12,341.50	12,920.84	2,748.41	15,669.25
1939	1,000.00	426.51	1,426.51	13,768.01	13,392.74	3,008.25	16,400.99
1940	1,000.00	628.70	1,628.70	15,396.71	12,481.34	3,084.62	15,565.96
1941	1,000.00	847.11	1,847.11	17,243.82	11,593.70	3,353.96	14,947.66
1942	1,000.00	908.92	1,908.92	19,152.74	14,062.49	4,721.45	18,783.94
1943	1,000.00	699.72	1,699.72	20,852.46	17,601.05	6,408.15	24,009.20
1944	1,000.00	754.80	1,754.80	22,607.26	20,585.91	7,960.26	28,546.17
1945	1,000.00	871.26	1,871.26	24,478.52	27,097.94	11,120.63	38,218.57
1946	1,000.00	944.85	1,944.85	26,423.37	24,967.98	10,739.63	35,707.61
1947	1,000.00	1,183.49	2,183.49	28,606.86	26,183.59	12,019.32	38,202.91
1948	1,000.00	1,513.40	2,513.40	31,120.26	27,160.53	13,553.21	40,713.74
1949	1,000.00	2,025.21	3,025.21	34,145.47	31,001.13	17,092.61	48,093.74
1950	1,000.00	2,663.25	3,663.25	37,808.72	40,209.77	24,839.08	65,048.85
1951	1,000.00	3,346.55	4,346.55	42,155.27	47,894.59	32,738.40	80,632.99
1952	1,000.00	3,627.88	4,627.88	46,783.15	53,707.95	39,938.28	93,646.23
1953	1,000.00	5,646.72a	6,646.72a	53,429.87	50,084.78	41,818.11a	91,902.89a

a Based on assumption that one-half of 1953 dividends were reinvested. Market values in 1953 are as of July 1.

Common stock investment, particularly in industrial shares, was once considered synonymous with gambling; it has now become so respectable that one is likely to forget how recently this change of opinion has come about. Forty years ago only a few economists and traders championed the cause of the common stock; thirty years ago the argument of common versus preferred and bonds was under way. . . . However, fifteen years ago, and again after World War II, the principal questions were not whether one should buy common stocks, but what and when to buy.

In their concluding chapter, Messrs. Eiteman and Smith remind readers that the investor in their study

. . . was assumed willing to invest funds in common stocks without recourse to advice, analysis, hunches, rumors, insider-tips, market positions, or trend techniques. He was willing to choose issues entirely on the basis of market volume, and he diversified his holdings only to the extent that the volume of sales in 1936 introduced the diversification.

Here is how the stocks were selected: the *Bank and Quotation Record* (published by *The Commercial & Financial Chronicle*) for January 8, 1937 was taken, and all common issues listed on the New York Stock Exchange and which had trading volumes of more than 1,000,000 shares in 1936 were included. This gave a list of 92 stocks representing 27 different industries.

You will see that this method avoids any trace of selection by value or virtue, either as market leaders (except in a volume sense) or by careful analysis of investment value. It left no room for favoritism due to hindsight, and it made no provision for selling or replacing any of the stocks held.

By making their selection in this way, the professors ruled out any "wise selection" of issues, and any possible benefits due to timing (getting in and out of the securities held when they seemed too low or too high). Only one thing remained: it was necessary to choose a period in which the market as a whole was about the same at the end as the beginning.

For this purpose the start was made on January 15, 1937. The study ended as of January 15, 1950. (It was purposely not continued because of the market rise following the later date.) It was decided that $1,000 would be invested in each of the 92 stocks each January 15, and all cash dividends received would be reinvested at the end of each year. Stock dividends were sold, and the proceeds reinvested along with the cash dividends. When *rights* (options to buy shares under some special arrangement) were received, they were exercised at the earliest possible date if funds were available. The only exceptions made to the "no changes in the list" policy were when mergers took place. Then shifts were made to the new securities offered in exchange for those held. Purchases of the new ones began as of the next regular investment date. Part of the text says:

If an investor selects common stocks by mechanical means, purchases them at arbitrarily predetermined dates during a period in which the market made no permanent gain, and still achieves a surprisingly high average annual yield, the results can scarcely be laid to any other factor than the high intrinsic merit of common stocks as an investment media.

In Table 5 you will see year-by-year results of this investment study.

One of the charts in this book shows the course of the Dow-Jones Industrial Average over the last 23 years. Although prices rose and fell many times, the trend was steadily upward at an average annual rate of 4.4%. Compared with the Dow for the period under study, the Michigan list did 27% better. Also, it did 72% better than the cost-of-living rise during the same years.

While the arithmetical average of the 92 stocks showed a gain of about 33% for each, there were wide differences in the performances of individual issues. The lowest stock, with

$15,000 invested over the period of study, had a market value of $10,275 at the end. The highest was worth $78,605.

TABLE 5.

	Paid In	Market Value
1937	$ 92,000	$ 92,000
1938	184,000	149,514
1939	276,000	255,589
1940	368,000	326,386
1941	460,000	412,083
1942	552,000	486,074
1943	644,000	690,273
1944	736,000	1,074,540
1945	828,000	1,580,878
1946	920,000	2,724,886
1947	1,012,000	2,169,708
1948	1,104,000	2,363,253
1949	1,196,000	2,525,266
1950	1,288,000	3,028,855

As regards income, here is a breakdown of the final results:

The investor had put into the 92 stocks	$1,288,000
Dividends had been reinvested for him amounting to	850,182
The stocks owned had gone up in price	890,673
Total	$3,028,855

The total dividends received were divided among the 92 stocks in widely different ways. Average was $9,241. The amounts actually paid by individual securities ranged from nothing to $21,000.

Here are the concluding words of the Michigan study:

Common stocks have become an integral part of our economic life. If our economy continues to grow and expand, as we believe it will, common stocks may be expected to continue the upward trend they have followed for fifty or more years. A program of purchasing common stocks at regular, stated intervals is obviously not the answer for all security buyers, but for a person interested in building a portfolio to obtain investment income, common stocks have much to offer.

In view of this comment, it is timely to examine this trend to common stocks by what might be termed professional investors. Some pages earlier, mention was made of the fact that Harvard University had turned over the management of its endowment fund securities portfolio to a management identified with the mutual fund field. Treasurer of the University is Paul C. Cabot, also Board Chairman of State Street Investment Corporation, a mutual fund with assets of more than $140,000,-000. State Street was organized in 1924. Shares are not now in distribution, but your investment dealer can quote them for you in the "over the counter" market. According to supply and demand, they sell at varying percentages above net asset value. Mr. Cabot has been Treasurer of Harvard for 9 years. As background for a look at the trend to common stocks, here is a table showing the University's distribution of investments by type on June 30 in each of several past years, in percentages.

	1929	1932	1948	1953	1957
Cash and U. S. Govt's	9.0	6.2	28.6	22.0	17.5
Other bonds	47.6	62.0	18.5	22.7	20.3
Preferred stocks	5.5	5.5	9.3	5.3	3.0
Common stocks	25.1	12.4	42.2	49.0	58.7
Real estate and mtgs.	12.8	13.9	1.4	1.0	0.5

The Harvard Endowment Fund stands as a tribute to skillful management. Throughout a difficult period of low money rates, 4% or better was consistently paid to the University. Market value on June 30, 1957 ($500,962,000) was more than $200,-000,000 above its historical cost. Income earned in 1957 was

$17,833,000, or about a 6% return on cost, and up from 4.4% in 1949. Income paid to the University was 5.2%—the highest in years.

As you see by the table, the most striking change in the last 9 years has been the steady increase in the percentage of investments in common stocks. This reflects the confidence the managers place in them as a medium of investment and as a means of maintaining the purchasing power of the University's income.

As of June 30, 1957, Harvard held investments of more than $2,000,000 each in 46 stocks, with others close to that figure. Largest in dollar value was Standard Oil of New Jersey, with $18,991,000. Here are the changes in percentages of common stock holdings by industry under Mr. Cabot's treasurership (all figures June 30):

	1948	1952	1953	1957
Railroad	1.5	3.3	5.5	3.0
Utilities	14.4	22.0	25.4	27.5
Banks	9.0	4.1	4.4	3.0
Insurance	10.1	10.3	10.2	9.6
Industrial	65.0	60.3	54.5	56.9

Since Mr. Cabot took over, the most marked change has been the increase in public utilities and oils. Lesser gains are found in steels, electrical equipment and paper at the expense largely of banks, retail trade, chemicals, and more recently, railroads. There has been a consistent policy of concentrating in fewer, larger holdings.

Late in 1957 there appeared in Vance, Sanders & Co.'s *Brevits* a study made by Boston Fund. It covered the endowment funds of 42 prominent universities and colleges with aggregate endowments of about $2.5 billion. Individual endowments ranged in size from $500,962,000 for Harvard to $3,793,241 for Bates College in Lewiston, Maine. Among endowments of more than

Our Mutual Fund Department sent me—thank goodness.

$100,000,000 were those of Yale, University of Chicago, North-western, Massachusetts Institute of Technology, University of Rochester, and Cornell. On an overall basis, the survey indicated that the 42 institutions had 32.0% in bonds and cash, 3.3% in preferred stocks, 55.1% in common stocks, 8.4% in real estate or mortgages and 1.2% in other forms of investment.

As of June 30, 1957, 31 of the 42 endowment funds had over 50% of their total assets in common stocks; 13 of them had 60% or more so invested and the largest proportionate holding (University of Delaware) was 85.5%.

From what we have seen in this chapter, two things seem plain. One is that common stocks have investment value. The other is that, if broadly diversified and purchased by the dollar cost averaging method, they offer rewards to the investor large or small.

But suppose you could add to the dollar cost averaging method an improvement which would remove doubtful holdings from your diversified list, and replace them with those of greater promise?

That is where mutual funds come in.

In the next chapter we shall see why the funds probably offer an ideal method of dollar cost averaging, and how they have simplified the mechanics of this practical way to invest in the securities of a broad list of American corporations.

5. Budgeted Investing

Your future financial problems. Why you need not be rich to buy mutual funds—Systematic investment plans—It is easy to start a plan, and to keep it up—What mutual fund owners are like—Combining mutual funds with insurance for an estate-building program.

Probably you know that, according to official records of the Bureau of Statistics in Washington, D. C., regardless of how much money they earned in their productive years, 95 out of every 100 men wind up broke and have to move in on their children, or depend on charity. Furthermore, these records show that only 1 man in 500 winds up with as much as $24,000. This figure takes into account all the billions of dollars people put into retirement insurance.

Nobody ever plans to be broke. It is like when you were in the army—it was always the fellow next to you who was going to get shot.

The way to do something about your financial future is to make the problems of that future a living, vital part of today's problems. Thrift is a wonderful virtue, somebody once said, and specially so in an ancestor. Why not act as your own ancestor? "Today's decision," one of the long-haired boys wrote years ago, "makes tomorrow's destiny."

You do not have to be rich to become an investor, any more than you have to be rich to buy a car, or a TV set. Unless you are rich, chances are you get your income weekly or monthly from your job. Does it not make sense to build your financial

58

future the same way? When you budget your investing, you are telling your money where to go, instead of wondering where it went. Moreover, you are paying yourself first instead of last.

Naturally, you will want something to shoot for in your investing plan. The simplest way to determine that goal is probably to figure how much income you want (in addition to your social security) when you become 65. U. S. Public Health Service figures show that if you (a male) live to be 65, your average life expectancy is more than 12 years, in which you must support yourself. Corresponding figure for a female is over 14 years.

If, after you retire, you want an income of $5,000 a year of today's dollar, for 12 years, you would need $60,000 if you used the money up as you went along, or $100,000 invested to bring you that mythical "sure 5%" if you plan to live on the income only.

These figures may well sound far beyond the means of the average wage earner, but at least a part of the financial goals shown can be reached by anyone who makes a serious effort to do so. Savings banks, annuities, and investment plans all have their uses in such a program. You need rainy day dollars provided by savings banks and insurance. These take care of your emergency and death needs. You need working dollars to earn you more income and give your capital a chance to grow. That is where systematic investment plans come in.

In other words, you need both dollar safety and the opportunity for growth in purchasing power. The most expensive thing you can do with your money is—*nothing!*

Back a few months ago a mutual fund dealer called on Ferd Nauheim, who teaches advertising at the American University in Washington, D. C. Taking the natural line of defense to which anyone solicited by a salesman turns, he said, "I have no money."

"The point is,' this dealer replied, "that you have money every week, but none of it stays home to earn more money. You have some insurance, and some government bonds. Couldn't you get along if you made $50 a month less than you get now?"

"There was the answer to my problem," Mr. Nauheim said later in discussing the experience with the editor of *Investor* magazine. "Through the year I get a fair flow of checks. Some are for interest, some for dividends, some for rent. They bother me because they represent surplus income. What I get from my regular work takes care of us nicely. The surplus income is fine, but it doesn't fill any immediate need.

"I could let those odds and ends of money accumulate, and then put them to work, but I never thought of them as big enough to be investment money. Because it comes in small amounts, it just melts away. That's why I wanted an investment plan—to build something substantial for the years ahead when I want to quit working. It's nice to dream about passing along a good solid financial base to the wife and children, too."

Not all buyers of mutual fund shares through systematic investing are fortunate in having extra income to salt away. For many, at first the monthly or quarterly investment means a struggle. Let us look at some other owners of budgeted investing plans, and see what their circumstances are.

In an advertisement run in late 1953 by the New York investment firm of Kidder, Peabody & Co. they headlined: "How to Start an Investment Program for as little as $200." Then, in a box headed "Our Customers," they gave these figures about people who have invested in funds through them:

75% are between 30 and 60 years of age
80% earn less than $10,000 yearly
72% invested initially less than $1,500
68% invested initially from savings
48% are small business proprietors, executives, office workers, salesmen, etc.
32% are doctors, lawyers, clergymen, teachers, nurses, etc.

In late 1957 a survey made by the National Association of Investment Companies showed that a typical systematic investment plan owner was aged 42 and had accumulated assets of about $5,600. This money was almost equally divided in thirds, with savings accounts and Savings Bonds representing 33.7%, mutual fund holdings 32.5% and individual corporate stocks held directly 33.8%. At the end of 1957 there were some 645,-000 systematic investing plans in operation. As to the "regular," or lump-sum purchaser of mutual fund shares, the NAIC survey showed him at age 54 owning assets of $21,500 divided among cash savings at 16.8%, individual corporate stocks held directly 60.3% and mutual fund shares 22.9%.

A questionnaire to which the Association received a gratifying response showed that diversification—the spreading of risk among many securities—was what half of both types of investors in mutual funds liked best about their holdings. The quality second in their choice was the professional investment management afforded by their ownership of shares, this being followed in their vote by convenience (absence of detail in handling their investments) and ready marketability.

Here are some figures showing the average starting investment and the average amount put in afterward under plans offered by five leading sponsors of mutual funds. A *sponsor* is an organization which creates shares and wholesales them through investment dealers.

Sponsor firm	*First investment*	*Average monthly investment*
Vance, Sanders & Co.	$560	$108
National Securities	780	78
Wellington Company	561	90
Calvin Bullock	500 plus	100 plus
North American Securities	400	70

North American Securities is the sponsor of Commonwealth Investment Company, and is generally credited with being first in the mutual fund field with systematic investing plans, in

1946. Since 1950, new Commonwealth plans opened have been over 5000 a year, and there are more than 40,000 in force.

Do not be alarmed if the first or monthly payments shown above look larger than those you might like to make. Many people are carrying budgeted investing plans on much less. In its magazine called *Changing Times,* the Kiplinger organization in Washington ran an article in June 1953 called "How to Pick an Investment Trust." Reproducing material from the annual chart book of mutual funds put out by Hugh A. Johnson, the article listed 63 funds of which 43 had systematic investing plans. Many more have been announced since that time.

Of the plans listed, minimum starting payments required ran from $20 to $250 and following payments from $10 up. As a matter of fact, most of the plans are flexible in the amounts you can put in, and the length of time you can go without making an additional payment without closing out your investment account. All the plans provide for automatic reinvestment of dividends, so that you can receive dividend checks if you want them, but unless you do, the dividends will be left in your account and reinvested in shares and fractional shares to help it grow.

Consult your dealer as to which plan is best suited to your needs. He will probably bring up again the matter of your particular objective (the amount of money you want to accumulate, or whether you are aiming at security, generous income, or profits). In a booklet called *The Custom-Made Mutual Fund* describing its offerings, the sponsor of Group Securities has this to say:

Few things are more personal than investing. Expert supervision is a dull tool until it is directed toward a specific goal—and if that supervision is to help you, that goal must be your own.

Consciously or unconsciously, each of us has one or more of these basic objectives in mind when we invest:

1. Stability of principal
2. Income

3. Growth of principal

The first step toward successful investing is to determine how important each of these objectives is to you—and to recognize the fact that each tends to be unfriendly one to another. To the degree we seek more stability in the value of our investments or in the rate of their return (yield), we correspondingly accept less possibility for their growth—and the reverse is also true. Obviously, an investment can grow only as it can change in value. Only to the degree that you can afford possible shrinkage in value should you seek growth, for the possibility of the one is always present with the other. Care in the selection of investments, and the timing of their purchase can tip the scale in your favor, but it is sound to assume that greater opportunities for growth entail greater risk.

Recognizing that, like so many things people want these days, mutual fund shares can be bought out of your family budget, let us be sure we do not confuse this method of investing with buying stocks on margin. Buying stocks on margin means that you go to a broker and put up whatever the required percentage is of the full cost of what you want to buy. The money you put up is your *margin*. At present, regulations demand that 50% or more of the full cost be put up. In 1929 it was 10%. Within recent years it has run as high as 75%.

As a current example, suppose you wanted to buy listed stocks worth $10,000. You would give the broker at least $5,000, and he lends you the rest. The margin corresponds roughly to the money you had to produce as a down payment when you bought your home, if you were not fortunate enough to pay the full price in cash.

When you start a systematic investing plan you do not say to the dealer, "I want $10,000 worth of X Fund shares. Buy them for me now and I will pay you so much each month." You state your intention of buying regularly and pay an agreed sum to open the account, which then remains an open account into which you can put more any time in the same way you would put money into a savings bank. Shares are purchased for you by the bank which handles the plan for the particular fund you have chosen. You receive regular statements from the bank, so you know at all times just how your account stands. You can keep this account open as long as you like, or close it whenever you wish and receive the shares you have bought, or cash representing their market value.

Let us run through the steps you would take in opening a systematic investment plan. First, you would fill out a form your investment dealer will provide. It states the amount with which you start, what you intend to invest each time thereafter, your name and address, and such other information as the sponsor and the bank may need.

Next you write out the check which starts your plan. Your dealer mails the form and the check to the sponsor, signing and dating his own authorization on it. This gives you official status (and an account number) with the bank. You will receive from the bank a receipt for your payment, and a confirmation showing the number of shares (including fractional shares) bought for you.

Meanwhile, the dealer will probably have given you an envelope to keep your receipts in, and a handy record form to keep track of your payments, although the bank will keep you up to date on these facts. Each time you make an investment you will receive a confirmation from the bank, with a statement showing the total number of shares you own, and a reminder of the date and amount of your next scheduled payment.

Quarterly dividends from investment income will be fully and automatically reinvested for you, as will any distributions from realized profits taken by your fund on securities it sells. Shares purchased by these reinvestments will be shown in the bank statements you get.

It should be understood that the bank has nothing to do with the management of the fund's portfolio, or with the investment policies. The bank simply acts as agent for the sponsor who creates the shares you buy, just as it may act as transfer agent, custodian, or trustee. When you leave your mutual fund shares with a bank in one of these investment plans, you of course save the expense of safekeeping your certificates. Also, for your convenience, the bank will accept payment for your account of (1) payroll deductions made by your employer, (2) amounts your personal bank sends periodically for investment at your instructions, or (3) dividend checks from corporations which you wish to have invested in your systematic plan. Consult your investment dealer as to how these time-saving arrangements can be made.

Here are a few of the questions often asked by investors who are thinking of starting such plans. They are asked and answered in a folder called *How to Make Prudent Investing a Habit*, issued by The George Putnam Fund.

Q: Suppose I sold a piece of property and had several thousand dollars to invest. Would it be permissible under your plan?

A: Certainly. One of the features of the plan is its flexibility. It is an open account.

Q: May I transfer my membership if I wish?

A: No. Memberships are not transferable. But if you wish to have somebody else own some or all of the shares you have accumulated, you may withdraw them from your account and register them in another name.

Q: Is all my money invested the day the bank receives it?

A: Yes. The amount in excess of the cost of full shares is used to buy a fractional share. All your money is always fully invested.

Q: May a membership be taken out in a child's name?

A: You may set up a simple trust—or act as Custodian—so that you can buy and hold shares in trust for a child. That, however, is something you should talk over with your investment dealer and your lawyer.

Q: If I need some money in an emergency, can I sell some of the shares in my account without giving up my membership?

A: Yes. Any number of shares you specify will be sold at the current asset value which, of course, will be more or less than their cost.

When you have been using this method of investing for some time, and have accumulated whatever amount of money you had in mind as a goal, you can leave your shares with the bank and receive regular dividends from them, or you can let the dividends continue to build up more principal for you. Or you may wish to withdraw the entire market value of your account in cash, or take the certificates representing your shares and keep them yourself.

When you start your investment plan you have avoided the two biggest risks there are in general, hit-or-miss investing. The first is buying stock in the wrong company. The second is buying the right stock at the wrong time. (You can be ahead of your time and lose a fortune, as many an investor has found to his sorrow. Investors who saw great possibilities in the transcontinental railroads during this country's early history found themselves holders of "first mortgages on a streak of rust.")

You have avoided these mistakes because you have decided to let professional supervision do your investment worrying and deciding for you. Furthermore, you will automatically receive the benefits of dollar cost averaging as described in the previous chapter. Whether or not you make your scheduled payments exactly on time, or omit a few, will make little difference over a period of years, but the main thing is to make as many, and make them as regularly, as you can.

There will be times when it will take courage, of course. Hard times may visit the United States again, as they did in 1930 to 1933. In those days the writer found conditions such in Greenwich Village that if he wanted to get his suit pressed and go to the movies in the same week, one or the other had to be done on time payments. In fact, things were so tough that if a young couple paid their rent for two consecutive months, the cops came around and wanted to know where they got the money.

It is such times that offer the greatest opportunities for the investor who will hang on to his plan and keep up his payments. Do not try to outguess the market. You will never be able to buy low and sell high, but under a systematic investment plan with dollar cost averaging you will buy high and also buy low. In a book published by Charles Scribner's Sons (*The Forgotten Fifty Billions*, by W. W. Craig and C. Gore), a chart shows that if a man had invested $100 a month in the Dow Jones Industrials starting at the top in 1929, the worst possible time, historically, he would have had a profit very early in 1935.

While the market declined from 381.17 to 42.84 (89%) this investor was ahead in early 1935 although the market was at 104.04 or 73% under the 1929 high. He had put in $6,400 and his investment was worth $6,545 not including any dividends or rights he had received, worth another $611.50.

If you decide to invest systematically, remember the cautions about dollar cost averaging given in Chapter 4. If you start a plan and have to give up making your investments in it, do not feel too badly. Other people have had the same experience. No cure-all for human experience, or human nature, has yet been discovered. At worst, if you have to stop investing, you can let the compounding factor keep rolling up your nest egg until you can start again. Or, if you have to close the account, chances are you will have a few hundred or maybe a few thousand dollars you never would have saved otherwise.

It is likely that if you have gone along this far with the budgeted investing idea you have said to yourself, "Sounds all right, but what if I die while I'm building this estate?"

A good question!

Some funds have plans with insurance features which you can use (with certain reasonable restrictions). As a discussion of this would be long and detailed, you are again referred to your investment dealer. He can tell you which funds have plans with insurance, which states they can be bought in, and how they work.

Many people, however, because of the restrictions on plans

with insurance, prefer to set up their own combinations of the two. Here is an example using shares in Fundamental Investors, plus term insurance.

John Blank was 35 years old in 1938, and was concerned about his financial future. He could put aside $100 a month. He had what he considered a suitable life insurance program once his children had grown up, and felt it was time for him to start investing in equity securities. But, he reasoned, if he should be removed, his family might be in want. So a combination of mutual fund shares plus a nonrenewable 15-year term insurance policy took care of that possibility.

This insurance cost him $169 a year, and he was covered for $18,613. The balance of his annual estate building money ($1,031) he put aside to buy shares in the fund. If he lived, he could sell his shares, or use them as collateral to borrow on at his bank, and his dividends would help pay the interest on his loan.

He chose to reinvest his dividends, which after the third year were large enough to pay his insurance premium had he wished to use them for that purpose. If he died, his family would have received cash of $18,613 from the insurance, plus a dividend-paying investment represented by the mutual fund shares he had bought up to that time. The results of his program are shown in Table 6.

As you see, John Blank wound up with a dividend-paying investment worth $42,863. The value of this investment will vary in the future, and it is not to be inferred that like amounts invested in the future will produce a similar or equal result. Dividends, which in the table amounted to $1,775 in 1952, may be greater or less in the following years.

Many people would like to have had such an experience. The only way to start is to start. Listen to George E. Swope, nationally known speaker on estate planning through funds and insurance. In closing a recent talk on investing in a broad cross section of American industry he said:

TABLE 6. JOHN BLANK'S PROGRAM

		If He Lived				If He Died	
Dec. 31	Cost of Insurance	Total of Cash Invested Annually in FI (cumulative)	Income Dividends Received and Reinvested (cumulative)	Total Cost of FI Shares	Liquidating Value of FI	Insurance Coverage	Total Insurance Coverage Plus Value of FI
1938	$ 169	$ 1,031	$ 13	$ 1,044	$ 1,186	$18,613	$19,799
1939	338	2,062	65	2,127	2,141	18,613	20,754
1940	507	3,093	172	3,265	2,899	18,613	21,512
1941	676	4,124	380	4,504	3,558	18,613	22,171
1942	845	5,155	633	5,788	5,614	18,613	24,227
1943	1,014	6,186	873	7,059	8,565	18,613	27,178
1944	1,183	7,217	1,168	8,385	11,705	18,613	30,318
1945	1,352	8,248	1,509	9,757	18,101	18,613	36,714
1946	1,521	9,278	1,799	11,077	17,331	18,613	35,944
1947	1,690	10,310	2,401	12,711	17,536	18,613	36,149
1948	1,859	11,341	3,355	14,696	18,697	16,613	37,310
1949	2,028	12,372	4,368	16,740	23,401	18,613	42,014
1950	2,197	13,403	5,760	19,163	30,517	18,613	49,130
1951	2,366	14,434	7,464	21,898	37,317	18,613	55,930
1952	2,535	15,465	9,239	24,704	42,863	18,613	61,476
1953 (Jan. 1)	2,535	15,465	9,239.	24,704	42,863a	None	42,863

a Includes $5,008 of securities profits distributions received and reinvested during period.

NOTE: All figures rounded to nearest dollar.

Here's my point. When does the time come when you sit down with your wife and say "Look, Dear, we've worked hard for the last twenty years. A lot of money has gone through our hands. When we look at our bank balance, there is mighty little there. We've been working for everybody but ourselves.

"Let's face it—we have only another fifteen or twenty years left. When they are gone it will be the Last of the Ninth, and we won't get to bat any more. By Golly, you and I are going to figure out some amount that isn't too hard for us to keep out of my paycheck and set it aside for ourselves. We're going to start owning a part in the businesses of all those fellows who have been getting all our money. Let them work for us!"

The literally thousands of such decisions that are being made each year is one reason for the growing investor acceptance of mutual funds and systematic investing plans. In early 1958 there were more than 639,000 such plans outstanding. During 1957, gross sales of fund shares ran around $1.4 billion. That is big business.

How is it regulated? What does government do to make sure the investor has all the necessary facts presented to him before he makes up his mind to buy shares, and how is he protected through the supervision of mutual fund companies and their operations? In Chapter 6 we shall see how Uncle Sam Looks On.

6. Uncle Sam Looks On

History of investment companies in the United States—Investment trusts—Fixed trusts—How federal and state regulation developed to curb early abuses of the investment company idea—Why the salesman must give you a prospectus, and what to look for in it— Literature and advertising which mutual fund retail dealers can and cannot use.

This chapter has to do with regulation of investment companies. It describes what they can and cannot do, what they must tell an investor who is considering buying their shares, the type of literature they must provide, what sort of advertising they are permitted to do, and so on. All this is for your protection.

Before such law making and enforcing can start there must be something to regulate, so it is interesting to see how investment companies developed in the United States, plunged from extreme popularity to a state of low public esteem, and through the years have found their way back to public favor to the extent that they (open-end and closed-end companies combined) had assets in early January, 1958 of more than $9.9 billion owned by over 3,364,000 investors. For year-by-year growth of the open-end companies (mutual funds) see Table 7.

Oldest investment company on record is Societe Generale de Belgique, founded by King William I of Belgium in 1822. As of early 1954 it was still in active operation and had assets of over $150,000,000. Scotland was the first country to adopt this form of investment in a general way. In Dundee a dozen or more such companies were formed between 1868 and 1875. Such companies flourished in Great Britain.

TABLE 7.   MUTUAL FUNDS 1940-1957[a]

December 31	Total Net Assets	Shareholders
1957	$8,714,143,000	3,110,392
1956	9,046,431,000	2,580,049
1955	7,837,524,000	2,085,325
1954	6,109,390,000	1,703,846
1953	4,146,061,000	1,617,032
1952	3,931,407,000	1,359,000
1951	3,129,629,000	1,110,432
1950	2,530,563,000	938,651
1949	1,973,547,000	842,198
1948	1,505,762,000	722,118
1947	1,409,165,000	672,543
1946	1,311,108,000	580,221
1945	1,284,185,000	497,875
1944	882,191,000	421,675
1943	653,653,000	341,435
1942	486,850,000	312,609
1941	401,611,000	293,251
1940	447,959,000	296,056

[a] Courtesy, National Association of Investment Companies.

In the United States the first such company was the Boston Personal Property Trust, founded in 1893 and still active in 1954 with about $9,000,000 in assets. The investment company idea did not become popular here until the late 1920's, when it became rampant.

Large investment banking houses (which at that time were still paying drawing accounts to their salesmen) were constantly scanning the financial horizon for new offerings. In the idea of investment companies they saw an almost unlimited supply of salable goods. Why, they asked themselves, if this sort of thing can be done in Great Britain, cannot it be done here?

They found that it could.

British and Scottish investment companies had then been operating for half a century. American investment bankers, adopting a sort of "It's the same deal but we can deal it better" approach, set up companies patterned after the foreign organizations. Shares in these companies, known as *investment trusts*, were offered to the public.

These American companies suffered from some of the same conditions which affected most of the early British trusts. Among these were:

1. They were started in periods of high prices for securities, so that the odds were against further large and continuing profits being made.

2. The bankers who brought out the shares in some cases created special shares of various types which they owned or on which they had options, so that they, rather than the investor who bought the common stock, benefited most.

3. The new companies, being so closely affiliated with the investment banking firms, were often used for purposes other than the sole objective of making all possible profits for the common shareholders.

If you care for a trip through the financial chamber of horrors created by these and other conditions of the late 1920's, read *Investment Trusts Gone Wrong*, written by John T. Flynn and published by *New Republic* in 1930. It details all the abuses of what are generally referred to as investment trusts. There are chapters on the pretrust days, early trusts and their financial advantages to their sponsors, holding companies, control of companies by others, intercompany dealings, and bank affiliates.

A gruesome picture is presented, and the reader of today should remember that the abuses mentioned have been outlawed by provisions of the Investment Company Act of 1940 and two preceding Securities Acts. An interesting part of Mr. Flynn's book is its conclusion, in which the author recommends the forming of groups much like the Investors Clubs of today, but with paid professional investment counsel or service. He gives as an example the State Street Investment Club, members of which put in $5 or more each month and secured their investment advice automatically by investing their money in "a well-known Boston investment trust."

Bear in mind that the subject companies in Mr. Flynn's book were formed shortly before or during 1929, when the securities markets were top-heavy but nobody had yet realized that fact. If you remember those days, you will recall that everyone from your bootblack up was watching the financial pages to see how much money he made in the stock market that day. It was before the securities bubble had burst. In fact, it was thriving and growing, getting bigger every day.

With the long rise in stock prices had come a speculative fever based on the idea that, "Those Wall Street fellows are certainly smart. If they can make such big profits for themselves, why shouldn't I let them take my savings and make some for me?" It was easy to sell shares in those fully managed companies known as investment trusts. "Fully managed" usually meant that almost complete discretion was left to the people who ran the companies, both in buying and selling securities for the portfolio and in operating the companies as well.

Many Wall Street Big Names hurried to climb aboard the investment trust band wagon. Shares were purchased eagerly and often rose rapidly in market price, even though no securities had been invested in by the managers. Following the lead of the larger organizations, lesser lights of the financial fraternity entered this new, lucrative field. Finally, not only in Wall Street but from coast to coast, almost everyone and his brother in the financial business had started an investment trust.

Beginning in October 1929 there developed the most serious decline in securities prices this country had ever seen. Good stocks sold off, along with the others. Per-share values shrank alarmingly overnight. Holdings of the trusts went down, along with securities in general. By 1931, a story going around the Street told of a financeer beseeching Saint Peter to let him enter the Pearly Gates. Refused, he sank to his knees, crying, "But Pete, I never started an investment trust."

With the speculative hangover came a rapid and violent distrust of Wall Street and other financial centers. "Maybe those fellows aren't as smart as we figured," reasoned the investor. "After this, they don't get any of my money. I'm putting it into the stocks of big, well-known companies that anyone will tell you are all right."

This marked the decline and fall of full management companies as represented by the ill-starred investment trust. The public wanted no more full management. However, it still had faith in American industry and its big name stocks.

Capitalizing on this idea that, "Good stocks are all right, but if I own them I don't want anybody changing them for me," there developed what was known as the *fixed trust*. In these, portfolios of 20 or more common stocks like American Telephone, Eastman Kodak, General Electric, Standard Oil of California, Union Pacific, and United States Steel were offered, usually 4 shares of each comprising a *unit*, which was trusteed with a bank or trust company. There was no portfolio supervision in the sense that securities would be replaced. Often the chief provision was that no stock would be sold unless it passed its dividend. In such a case, the proceeds from the stock were divided among the shareholders on the next (usually semiannual) distribution date. This made fine big dividends, but usually the investor had no idea that his yield was being boosted by a return of part of his own money.

"That's the stuff. Nobody's going to fiddle with my list of holdings any more," cried thousands of American investors who in 1930 and 1931 put their dollars into such shares.

Had the creators of these fixed trusts started two or three

years later, they probably would have been honored by statues in every public square, as stocks started an abrupt rise in 1933. But like so many geniuses, they were ahead of their times. The fixed trust shares also declined in price, despite the fine selection of blue chip portfolio stocks.

So the pendulum swung, from full management with practically no restrictions to "refrigerated management," or no management at all. Was there a reasonable, practical middle ground combining able initial selection with competent supervision?

The answer to that question marked the development of what are called *open-end investment companies*, or *mutual funds*. There are three federal acts under which they operate, plus two other forms of regulation. Of these two, one is the security rulings of the various states, called *blue sky laws*, and the other is the *statement of policy*, about which more later on in this chapter. Blue sky laws are local to the state, of course, and are promoted by the commissioner in charge of that branch of regulation. Your investment dealer knows the laws of your state, and naturally will not offer you a fund not qualified for sale there.

The three federal acts under which investment companies operate are:

1. The Securities Act of 1933. This governs the issuance and sale of securities. Shares in mutual funds, although they are in continuous supply, are considered new securities.

2. The Securities and Exchange Act of 1934. This applies in part to open-end as well as closed-end investment companies.

3. The Investment Company Act of 1940.

All these three acts are designed in the public interest. Most directly affecting those considering mutual funds is the last.

Previous to 1940, the status and the future of the mutual fund business were both uncertain. No industry code existed, and there were trade practices which, while they in no way worked against the benefits to the investor in owning mutual fund shares, were a sore thorn in the flesh to sponsors and wholesalers carrying on a legitimate business in the distribution of such shares. Investment Trusts were still a favorite target of scarehead columnists who, when they felt uninspired to write on other topics, could always reach into the barrel and come up with 1929. As regards educational work aimed at letting the public know what mutual funds were, and how they operated, the surface had hardly been scratched. Pioneering in this were three organizations who had started funds well before 1929. State Street Investment Company (previously mentioned in connection with Harvard University) was then in distribution. The Parker Corporation had created Incorporated Investors, and the predecessor of the present Vance, Sanders & Company sponsored Massachusetts Investors Trust, oldest and largest open-end company distributed in the United States by members of the National Association of Securities Dealers.

It was natural for both the federal government and the investment company sponsors to want the situation clarified. After a 5-year study the Securities & Exchange Commission had proposed an Investment Company Act under which, if passed in its original form, investment companies would be so restricted that they could not have grown as they have in the past decade, and it is even doubtful that many of them would have survived.

In a spirit of cooperation with the Commission, heads of various investment companies, both open and closed-end, went to Washington and gave ungrudgingly of their time to work out, with the Commission, a bill designed to prevent abuses but realistic in recognizing the needs of the business. A bill satisfactory to all parties concerned was written, and passed both Houses of the Congress without a single negative vote. Officially known as H.R. 10065, its short title (Sec. 52) is "Investment Company Act of 1940." Approved by Congress on August 22, it became effective November 1 of that year.

Something should be said here about the National Association of Investment Companies, which grew out of the joint effort just described. John M. Sheffey, former Executive Secretary of the Association says,

Previous to the Senate hearings which preceded passage of the Act, the people in the business barely knew each other. At first, open-end companies joined in one group and closed-ends in another, for their own protection. However, in the discussions and hearings in Washington they discovered a common basis for affirmative action. Both groups wanted sound regulation.

Upon enactment of the Investment Company Act, the Securities Commission and the industry realized that there remained the important task of drafting rules and regulations, the registration statement, and other forms. It was of paramount importance that some investment company group be set up to maintain contact with the Commission as the various regulatory provisions of the Act were put into effect.

Such a committee, established in 1940, grew into what is now the National Association, acting as a central agency through which investment companies may express their views to the Commission. Since 1941 it has joined other organizations in proposing amendments to securities legislation, efforts to simplify prospectuses and registration forms for both types of investment companies, and opposition to proposed increased charges for the privilege of being regulated. Also, the Association has improved the tax status of the companies both from the company standpoint and from that of the investor who owns shares. It has been an important factor in having favorable legislation enacted in many important states, and is actively concerned with federal and state legislation regarding legal investments for trustees, fiduciaries, retirement plans, and various types of institutional investors.

Each quarter the Association releases official figures on assets and sales of investment companies and the number of their shareholders. It has collaborated with the Brookings Institution and the New York Stock Exchange in surveys of stockholders, and has furnished speakers or representatives for annual meetings of the Investment Bankers Association, the National Association of Securities Administrators (state blue sky commissioners), mutual fund conventions, and economic and other Congressional committees.

It cooperates with authors and publishers of books and articles on investment companies by checking manuscripts and providing factual information, keeps its members informed of important developments in their field, and answers inquiries from members, the press, professors and students, and the general public. In 1953, under the chairmanship of Mr. Henry Vance of Vance, Sanders & Company, a public relations program for the Association was formulated and proposed to members. Both closed and open-end members, representing 90% of total assets of all members, supported this program, which began to operate in 1954 under a committee consisting of top executives from 6 open-end fund sponsor firms and 1 closed-end company.

This background is helpful in understanding the Investment Company Act of 1940, which requires that investment companies must register with the Securities & Exchange Commission for regulation by the Act. They are defined as companies engaged in, or proposing to engage primarily in "the business of investing, reinvesting, or trading in securities." [Sec. 3 (a) 1.]

An "open-end company" means a management company "offering for sale or having outstanding any redeemable security of which it is the issuer." [Sec. 5 (a) 1.]

A registration statement furnishes to the federal government all information it believes necessary to aid investors in selecting securities. Furthermore, an open-end investment company must furnish periodic reports to the Commission. A mutual fund must live as publicly as a sparrow.

For willful violations of the Act, penalties are provided up to fines of $10,000 and sentences of not more than two years in prison. Its provisions cover the activities of retail distributors of mutual fund shares as well as those of the issuing companies or sponsors.

To start offering shares in a mutual fund there must be assets of at least $100,000. In the early days, too many funds were started on shoestrings. All shares must have equal voting rights, thus doing away with abuses which once made it possible for insiders to benefit materially at the expense of public holders.

A fund cannot issue securities which would come ahead of its common stock. It can borrow money provided [Sec. 18 (f) 1] that "immediately after any such borrowings there is an asset coverage of at least 300% for all borrowings of such registered company." This ratio must be maintained. In other words, for each dollar the company borrows, it must have $3 in assets, and must keep borrowings and assets at not less than that proportion. Few mutual funds actually borrow, but this provision should be understood. Your investment dealer can tell you which the borrowing funds are, and explain to you their thinking which leads to this activity.

Very important is the provision of the Act that a fund cannot change its policy without a consenting vote of shareholders. That is, a stock fund could not suddenly decide to invest only in bonds, or a balanced fund could not overnight become a stock fund unless (1) such rights were detailed in the registration statement, or (2) were approved by stockholder vote.

A fund cannot trade on margin, or engage in short sales. A *short sale* is selling something you do not own but promise to deliver in the future either at a specified time or at your convenience. For instance, if you promised your brother-in-law to get him two good seats for some Broadway show for a certain performance, figuring you could pick them up easily, you would be "short" the two tickets until you had made delivery. Stocks are often sold by speculators on this basis. In such cases the broker, acting for his customer, borrows the certificates representing the shares and delivers them to the broker to whom the short sale was made. The customer figures he can buy back similar shares at less than his selling price, and sometimes he can.

The actual securities owned must be held for a fund by a bank or a member firm of a national securities exchange. Any official of the fund having access to the securities must be bonded.

Funds must make official reports to their shareholders at least semiannually, and such reports must be audited by independent accountants. Use of the particular accounting firm must be approved by stockholder vote. These reports show certain required material such as gain or loss in net assets during the period under review, and usually contain a letter from an official of the fund commenting on the economic scene and the progress the fund has made or what its investment thinking at the time may be.

Many of the reports are workmanlike black-and-white jobs, but others are illustrated and make bountiful use of color. Among these are the reports on National Securities Series sponsored by National Securities & Research Corporation. At the annual Awards Dinner conducted by *Financial World* magazine, National's report has more than once captured first place in the investment companies division.

In the Investment Company Act it is provided that investment management contracts must be approved by stockholder vote. These contracts run for not to exceed 2 years and are renewable only with stockholder approval. Stockholders must also approve the election of directors of a fund, except for short interim terms to fill vacancies.

Two interesting provisions of the Act cover the possibilities of a fund going overboard by investing too much in some situation which seems to be of unusual promise. Both are in Sec. 5 (b) (1). The first limits the initial investment made by the fund to an amount not greater than 5% of its total assets. This is done to avoid the possible overenthusiasm of fund managers for some situation developing to a point costly to the shareholders. If a fund makes a purchase, and that purchase advances in value so that it represents more than 5% of the fund's assets, that is permissible.

The other provision limits a fund to holding not more than 10% of the securities of any company. This does away with the buying for control which was sometimes overdone in the 1929 era. These two provisions tend to insure built-in diversification of holdings.

Neither the Securities & Exchange Commission, nor the bank which holds a fund's securities in safe-keeping, is in any way the manager of that fund, or supervisor of its practices or policies. The Commission acts purely as a regulatory body. The bank acts as custodian or trustee only.

When a salesmen or dealer makes you an offering of mutual fund shares, he must comply with the law by giving you what is called a *prospectus*. This is a sort of junior registration statement, and contains much of the same material which the fund has filed in Washington. It states the objective of the fund, tells you the connections of its officers, contains financial statements of various sorts, shows how the asset value per share and the offering price are figured, how shares are redeemed, and many other features. Some of these prospectuses are pretty dry reading, others have been written in terms of investor interest as well as compliance with the law. Dry or otherwise, the salesman must give you one when he offers shares to you, whether you buy them or not. Before you buy, you should read it. In the prospectus you have sufficient information on which to decide whether or not shares in that particular fund are what you want. On other pieces of literature the salesman gives you, you will find a statement to the effect that it is "not authorized for use without previous or concurrent delivery of a prospectus."

This brings up the whole question of literature on mutual funds: what the salesman can and cannot tell you, and why. To understand how this works, let us look at the National Association of Securities Dealers, Inc., formed years ago as a voluntary body to regulate the entire investment business from within. Executive Secretary of NASD is Wallace Fulton, with headquarters in Washington, D. C. The NASD official most closely identified with and interested in mutual funds is Raymond Moulden, Secretary of the Investment Companies Committee of the Association.

Any piece of literature proposed to be used by a fund or a retailer in connection with sales work—and this includes reprints from newspapers and magazines, the regular reports of the funds, and any material such as booklets or circulars they produce—must comply with what is known as the *statement of policy* before it can be given to investors, prospective or otherwise. For instance, if a retailer of mutual funds wanted to give you a copy of this book he should ascertain if it had been so cleared.

Mr. Moulden's work is guided by regulations laid down in this statement of policy. He screens (approves, edits, or disapproves) material proposed to be used. As you will see, the provisions of the statement are designed to prevent overenthusiasm in offering mutual fund shares. It was issued by the Securities & Exchange Commission in 1950. Broadly speaking, it requires that any recommendation of a fund, oral or written, shall not contain an untrue or misleading statement of a material fact, nor must it omit any material fact necessary to an accurate appraisal of that particular fund. The National Association of Securities Dealers, Inc. administers the statement of policy (revised late in 1957) for its members.

The statement lays down specific manners in which certain information may be given. If a fund wanted to show its performance record, it could not take any period of time it happened to like. According to the statement it would have to take the entire life of the fund, or a period of the most recent ten years. If periods of longer than ten years but not the whole life are shown, they shall consist of fifteen or twenty years or other multiples of five years.

Other provisions of the statement of policy forbid promises of generous yields or representations of rates of return except in accordance with certain prescribed formulas, possibilities of profits being mentioned without also mentioning possibility of loss, the warnings you have already read about dollar cost averaging, and other phases of mutual fund investment where benefits might be inferred or implied without actually being promised. Also it is required, in any piece of literature not carrying a mention of the specific sales charge of the fund offered, that there be included in the text in a separate paragraph in type as large as that used generally in the body of the piece this statement: "There is a sales charge to the investor included in the offering price of shares of this company. For details thereof and other material information see the prospectus."

When the statement of policy became effective, hundreds of thousands of dollars worth of expensive sales literature had to be thrown away. This included many reprints of newspaper and magazine articles which did not conform to statement requirements. However, reasonably long advance notice was given distributors of the funds, and the move toward uniformity in literature has put all sponsors on the same footing, as well as attempting to protect investors from exaggerated claims as to what funds could or might do for them.

Much the same restrictions as cover sales literature also apply to individual fund advertising. The law originally stated that an advertisement might only "identify the security, state the price, and tell where a prospectus might be obtained." These regulations apply only to offerings of specific funds—not to recommendations of funds in general.

In this latter classification, an advertisement run by Kidder, Peabody & Co. in *The New York Times* said in part:

More and more people are finding that Mutual Funds offer a prudent way to invest for the future. Mutual Funds are managed by qualified professionals who seek well-defined results. Your investment in Mutual Funds can represent an ownership in 50 or 100 or more selected securities—a cross section of American industry—to spread your risk.

On the same day, in the *New York Herald Tribune*, Bache & Co. advertised:

Mutual Funds can help you build your financial future. There's a Fund for every purpose, every pocketbook. Extra shares can be accumulated as you want them. Dividends can be automatically reinvested if you wish.

So Uncle Same looks on, his intention being to see that his nieces and nephews who have money to invest and who may be considering mutual funds have sufficient and not misleading information to go on. Those who decide to look further into the subject will find in the next chapter some helpful ideas on how to benefit most from fund ownership, and how holdings of shares can be made most useful and rewarding.

7. Getting Most from Your Fund

Your share of the profits your mutual fund makes; where they come from and how you get them—What to do with them and why they should be reinvested—Do not waste your capital—An actual 10-year experience with and without the reinvestment of realized profits distributions—Protecting a widow or a minor by use of a revocable trust—Other conveniences you get in owning funds.

There are two important subjects to be covered, in considering how you can benefit most through the ownership of your mutual fund:

1. What to do with your capital gains distributions
2. The special investor conveniences of various kinds

Let us begin by understanding just what capital gains distributions are, and where they come from. A capital gains distribution, which you receive from your fund sometime during its fiscal year and usually at the end of that year, is simply your share of the realized profits the fund has taken since it last paid such a distribution. There is no certainty that such distributions will be paid.

Ordinarily, when paid, you get them at a year end because it is hard for a fund management to tell early in the year just how its realized profits (from securities sold) are going to compare with its realized losses. To be reasonably sure, the management waits until it has a definite idea of just how it will stand at the year end. It then sends you a notice saying that you will receive, on a certain date, a capital gains distribution. Usually, you have the option of taking this distribution in cash or in shares of the fund which you will receive at net asset value (that is, you get them without paying any sales charge).

Whether or not your fund would like to make these capital gains distributions has little to do with its decision, for the tax status of investment companies makes it better for both the fund and the shareholders if they are paid out.

The Federal Internal Revenue Code specifically provides for special treatment of open-end mutual funds which relieves them of substantially all federal income taxes. To secure this tax exemption, a fund must pay out 90% or more of its net investment income to its shareholders. If part of the income is retained, it is taxed at the regular corporate rates. This applies to net investment income, or dividends paid to the fund by the stocks in its portfolio.

If capital gains are not paid out to shareholders they are subject to a 25% tax. With these provisions in mind, most funds avoid payment of federal income taxes by paying out both net investment income and capital gains.

Harry I. Prankard, II, President of Affiliated Fund and of American Business Shares, in his interesting and helpful pamphlet called *Understanding Capital Gains Distributions*, puts it this way:

Dividends from net investment income represent true income to the shareholder, the same as the usual dividends he might receive from other types of corporations. They are spendable in the hands of the shareholder like income from any other source. They need not be reinvested to maintain the shareholder's capital and earning power in the company and if they are reinvested they add to his capital, the same as new money from any other source.

Distributions of net profits realized from the sale of securities are not income to the shareholder. The Federal income tax law, for example, taxes such profits, not as income but as capital gains, and at effective rates of one-half or less of the tax rates on ordinary income. They are not recurring and should not be spent as income by the shareholder. They must be reinvested to maintain the shareholder's capital and earning power in the company.

The Federal tax law recognizes that an investment company is a conduit between its shareholders and the companies in which its funds are invested. Therefore the law attempts to put the shareholder in the same position, from an income tax standpoint, as he would be in if he owned the securities of those companies directly. It does not tax the investment company on its net investment income or on its realized profits as long as they are distributed, but instead taxes the shareholders receiving them. This means that the shareholder pays substantially the same taxes as if he managed his own investments and, like the investment company, realized profits by the sale of securities whenever it seemed that the money could be better employed in other securities.

As a result of this method of taxation, whether the shareholder receives a capital gain distribution in cash or in stock it is reportable, for Federal income tax purposes, as a long-term capital gain (a gain from the sale of capital assets held for more than six months). This is true whether or not he held the shares on which he received the distribution more or less than six months prior to the receipt of the distribution.

Since the distribution represents capital gain rather than ordinary income, it is subject to tax at no more than one-half the rate that would be paid on the same amount of ordinary income. If the shareholder's highest rate, for example, is 34%, the effective rate of taxation on a capital gains distribution is ordinarily only 17%.

Should this sound complicated to you, do not be alarmed. The fund you own will make it simple by supplying you with all the facts necessary in making out your tax returns, whether federal or state. Its sponsor will see that the information is in your hands in plenty of time for proper use.

Regulatory authorities insist that the funds identify the source of all dividends or distributions paid to you. The reason goes way back to the fixed-trust days, when shareholders often received part of their own money back but spent it under the mistaken impression that it was income. Now you will be told what part of your check is true income and what part you should treat as a return of part of your capital.

That brings up the question of what you should do with these capital gains distributions, which are in effect a return of part of your money.

Look at it this way. Suppose your Cousin Frank comes to you in desperate need of $100. You want to help him, so you draw that amount out of your savings bank account and lend it to him. Cousin Frank is not the type that ever has $100 at any one time, but he is an earnest soul with a sense of obligation to you, and as he earns the money he pays you back $5 or maybe $10 at a time. You take these small parts of your capital, but instead of putting them back in the savings bank account you spend them. Cousin Frank has paid you, but you still have $100 less in your savings account than when the loan was made.

Much the same sort of thing happens when you take a capital gains distribution in cash instead of stock. On the ex-dividend date the offering price of the shares is reduced by the amount of the distribution. If you take shares instead of cash, you will have just as many dollars at work in the fund as you had before the distribution. If not, your interest in the fund is reduced by whatever number of dollars the shares you could have taken are worth. Taking a capital gains distribution in cash leaves you in the same position as if you had not received the distribution but had sold some of your shares to raise the same amount of money.

If you take the capital gains distribution in stock you will have 2 stock certificates (your new one and the old one) instead of one, but both together will have the same value and earning power that your old certificate had before the distribution. When you elect to take a capital gains distribution in stock, if there are fractional shares to be considered the fund will send you a check for any amount of money over what is required to buy the largest number of shares your distribution will purchase.

An actual illustration of the difference between investing and not investing capital gains distributions will be of interest. The chart opposite was furnished by The Parker Corporation, investment manager and general distributor of Incorporated Investors (founded in 1925 and dedicated to "long term growth of capital and income") and of Incorporated Income Fund (organized in 1954 to serve investors wanting "income now"). The chart shows you the assumed experience of a $10,000 investment from 1948 to 1957, inclusive. The shareholder elected to take in cash his dividends from investment income, but he was wise enough to accept his capital gains distributions in additional shares.

Neither the chart nor Table 8 (below) is to be taken as an indication of future performance. It should be remembered that equity prices in 1957 were generally higher than in 1948. Table 8 shows results at the end of the period assuming that the investor took both his investment income dividends and his capital gains distributions in cash.

TABLE 8.

Year Ended	Dividends Taken in Cash	Asset Value At Year End
1948	$ 574	$ 8,520
1949	564	9,541
1950	610	12,321
1951	599	13,673
1952	548	14,515
1953	528	13,214
1954	549	20,077
1955	607	24,311
1956	663	25,255
1957	638	17,883
	$5,880	

ILLUSTRATION OF AN ASSUMED INVESTMENT OF $10,000 IN SHARES OF INCORPORATED INVESTORS

With Capital Gains Distributions Accepted in Additional Shares

The chart below covers the period from January 1, 1948 to December 31, 1957. This period was one of generally rising common stock prices. The results shown should not be considered as a representation of the dividend income or capital gain or loss which may be realized from an investment made in the Fund today.

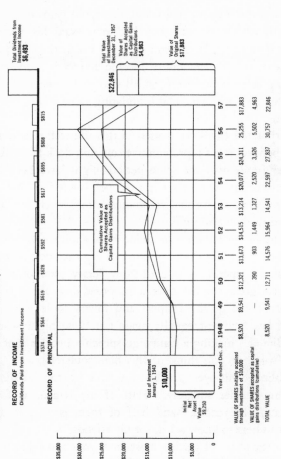

RECORD OF INCOME
Dividends Paid from Investment Income

RECORD OF PRINCIPAL

Total Dividends from Investment Income **$6,493**

Cost of Investment January 1, 1943 **$10,000**

Initial Net Asset Value **$9,250**

Total Value of Investment December 31, 1957 **$22,846**

Value of Shares Accepted as Capital Gains Distributions **$4,963**

Value of Original Shares **$17,883**

Year ended Dec. 31	1948	49	50	51	52	53	54	55	56	57
Dividends	$374	$564	$619	$678	$592	$581	$617	$695	$808	$815
VALUE OF SHARES initially acquired through investment of $10,000	$8,520	$9,541	$12,321	$13,673	$14,515	$13,214	$20,077	$24,311	25,255	$17,883
VALUE OF SHARES accepted as capital gains distributions (cumulative)	—	—	390	903	1,449	1,327	2,520	3,526	5,502	4,963
TOTAL VALUE	8,520	9,541	12,711	14,576	15,964	14,541	22,597	27,837	30,757	22,846

Cumulative Value of Shares Accepted as Capital Gains Distributions

Initial net asset value is the amount received by the Fund after deducting from the cost of the investment the sales commission as described in the prospectus.

No adjustment has been made for any income taxes payable by stockholders on capital gains distributions accepted in shares. The dollar amounts of capital gains distributions accepted in shares were: 1950 — $383; 1951 — $461; 1952 — $476; 1953 — $8; 1954 — $337; 1955 — $379; 1956 — $1,621; 1957 — $1,400. Total — $5,065.

Chart 1

Not shown in Table 8 are capital gains distributions totalling $4,490 made up as follows: 1950-$383, 1951-$446, 1952-$446, 1953-$8, 1954-$306, 1955-$337, 1956-$1,416, 1957-$1,148.

Suppose the investor had taken his capital gains distributions in additional shares, and also had reinvested his investment income dividends. At the end of 1957 his total cost ($10,000 plus the cumulative amount of income dividends reinvested and including sales commissions on all shares so purchased) would have been $18,202. His total liquidating value would have been $33,579.

Incorporated Investors is used in this illustration because the author believes it is a representative common stock fund. Records of other funds over the same period might have been less or more rewarding. At no place in this book is any fund mentioned in the sense of a personal recommendation—each has its purpose and its own philosophy.

Should he be tempted to influence a choice between them, the author would be in the position of a great uncle of his who once ran for sheriff in a small New Jersey community where there was great conflict over a proposed law about shooting squirrels. Some of the farmers and townspeople were 100% for the law, the rest equally against it. One night when old Uncle Ike was making a campaign speech a heckler shot out at him: "What do yuh think of this here squirrel law?"

Ike blinked his eyes, grabbed the table in front of him, and faced his heckler squarely. "Half of my friends is for that there law," he roared, "and half of them is agin it. I want every man here to know—I'm for my friends!"

The next phase of getting most from your fund which might be discussed is the various special conveniences of securities ownership available through this packaged investing. Few of us may have enough bond coupons and dividend checks to handle to make the job a burden, but it should be repeated that the owner of securities through a fund saves himself that burdensome detail, and also the chore of keeping track of individual dividend payments as well as the certificates themselves.

Perhaps the most valuable asset a fund owner has is the fact that he can pass along to his widow or his heirs a ready-made investment advisory service, already working automatically for them, and without the necessity of filing many forms in many states where individual securities are owned.

Many people are in positions where they would like to protect a wife or some relative, but do not wish to give up, during their own lifetime, the income from the securities which would furnish such protection. In many such cases, a revocable living trust provides the answer. To be sure your desires will be met, such a trust must be mentioned in your will.

For instance, a father wishes to leave securities to his son, but is doubtful about the boy's ability to manage a portfolio of stocks and bonds, or perhaps feels that the lad might be tempted to have a fling once he got hold of the proceeds of the gift. The father can wisely leave shares in a mutual fund (solving the problem of portfolio management) in a revocable living trust. The fund shares would belong to the father and he would receive the income to the time of his death, or such earlier time as he might elect. Meanwhile, the boy would know nothing of the arrangement unless the father wanted to tell him. The fund shares themselves could be left with a local bank, which would charge a nominal sum for custodianship. On the death of the father, the son would receive the income only.

The same sort of arrangement might name wife as beneficiary under such a revocable trust. Should the husband die, she would receive the income from the shares but would have no problem of portfolio management, nor would she be the prey of ill-intentioned friends or relatives who wanted to impose upon her. All she would have to do would be to point out that she could not touch the principal amount, but received the income only.

Writing on the subject of living trusts in *The Commercial & Financial Chronicle* of October 22, 1953, John Dutton summarized other features of such a trust where the widow is beneficiary:

It would relieve her of worry because she could depend upon continuous income and the substantial nature of her investment.

It would also save her the expense of putting that portion of her estate through probate and the legal fees involved. Such fees average around 7½% on any sizable sum and in some cases will be more where there is real estate.

It would save disclosure of that portion of the estate which was left under a revocable living trust, and the income would continue on without interruptions and delays which would be incurred if the estate were left outright to the wife and she had to go through the long involved court procedure before it finally passed to her.

No inheritance or gift taxes are saved by the use of such trusts, but their simplicity appeals to many investors who are looking ahead to the time when others may be enjoying the money they have accumulated.

Any person wishing to set aside funds for another can sign such a declaration of trust. Copies go to the fund, the donor (maker of the trust), and the person named as trustee, who may be the donor or some other person. The beneficiary may be a minor. The trustee may buy, sell, invest, and otherwise control the property, and the trust may run until a minor beneficiary reaches a specified age, or until the donor decides to revoke (cancel) the trust.

A successor trustee may be named to serve should the original trustee die; often one parent is named as trustee and the other as successor trustee. The donor pays taxes on the income received from the trust.

Your investment dealer can no doubt furnish you with sample trust forms. You should consult him, and probably your lawyer, to be sure you are complying with the regulations in force in your state.

There are also irrevocable declarations of trust, but these are in less frequent use. In its folder called *Junior Partner* which

Daddy, I want one with Checks Appeal.

deals with the subject of living trusts for minors, Commonwealth Investment Company says:

Under this arrangement (the irrevocable trust) the shares are registered in your name (or that of a person you name) as trustee, and in this capacity you can sell the shares and reinvest the proceeds. Because the declaration is irrevocable, however, you cannot terminate the arrangement once it has been made. The funds set aside, whether invested or not, must be held in trust for the child. In view of this relative inflexibility, it is recommended that persons setting up irrevocable trusts involving substantial sums consult their legal and tax advisers.

There is much to be said in favor of this method of protecting the future of minors in whose financial welfare you have an interest. As one semiphilosopher expresses the idea: "If your children are going to put their trust in riches, put your riches in trust for them."

Now, as to the personal convenience of the mutual fund shareholder. We have already touched upon the idea of buying 3 funds instead of 1, and selecting them so that a dividend check will be due each month, all around the calendar. Your dealer can help you with this selection, perhaps even giving you funds under 3 different managements. The number of dollars you receive each month will vary, just as the income of the funds varies, but it is a fact that no open-end mutual fund has ever missed making a regular distribution of investment income.

We have also mentioned the idea of having dividends from other corporations whose stocks you own sent direct to your mutual fund for investment. Your dealer can give you forms to fill out for this purpose, or instruct you as to the proper letter to write. When, let us say, you have written to the United States Steel Corporation telling it to send your dividend checks to X Fund, each time this is done you will receive an acknowledgment from the fund.

Another method of automatic investing is to have your employer (who may be a corporation, or Uncle Sam if you are in the Armed Forces) make payroll deductions for you and send them to your fund. In the case of some funds this is not practical because of their minimum required first payment, but with others it can be done easily. The Axe-Houghton Funds, for instance, under a payroll-deduction arrangement waive the initial payment requirement and will accept monthly amounts as low as $25. Additional amounts may be invested whenever the plan owner wishes to do so.

While on the subject of payroll deductions, it should be pointed out that many corporations encourage investment by their employees, and in some cases give them a choice of what they will buy. An excellent example is the Socony Mobil Oil Co., which handles an investment account in which the employee may choose between U. S. government bonds, Socony Mobil stock, or shares in any one of a number of qualified mutual funds.

Also there is a decided trend by corporations to supplement their insurance pension plans by stock investment plans, so that the employee may use either, or both. A leader in this field was the College Retirement Equities Fund established by Teachers Insurance and Annuity Association. This Equities Fund (to provide a chance for money to grow and thus combat rising living costs) was two years old when this book was first published. Already (early 1954) 400 colleges, universities, and other educational institutions had made it available to their staff members.

An early industrial equity annuity plan was that of the Long Island Lighting Company, which operates a portfolio combining fixed-income securities with common stocks. A combination of insurance annuities and mutual fund investment has been announced by the Post and Lester Company, a television and electrical appliance distributor in Hartford. A bank-trusteed arrangement provides an equity annuity based on common stocks as a supplement for its insurance company annuities, payments being about equally divided between the two.

"For five years we had been looking for a plan especially designed for the small concern," said Mr. P. J. Carr, Treasurer of the Company. "The standardized features of the balanced retirement system gave us the advantage of actuarial and economic advice we needed within our budget. The combination of an equity and a fixed-dollar annuity gives our employees better assurance of security in their old age regardless of whether we have long-term inflation, level prices, or deflation."

Announcement of the Post and Lester plan included the statement that its initial purchases for the equity annuity account would be shares of mutual funds.

For the individual investor, shares in mutual funds make exceptionally welcome birthday or Christmas gifts—"gifts that keep on giving" as dividend checks are received. Just as many a child has been prompted to become a saver through the deposit for him at birth of a few dollars in a bank, many have become investors because of gifts of mutual fund shares.

A novel use for such shares has been mentioned in the sales literature of Managed Funds, of St. Louis. One of their dealers had a client who had no success at all in teaching his son the value of money. Money, to the boy, was "just something your old man has." To make his son more conscious of the responsibility of money management, the father bought him enough shares of a mutual fund to give him an income equal to the allowance he had been receiving. Each quarter, when the dividend check comes in, the father explains to the boy that the dollars must last until the next check, and impresses on him the value of financial planning.

Besides discussion of new conveniences and advantages through mutual fund ownership, one subject which comes up at every national Mutual Fund Convention deals with the right— or wrong—time to buy shares. In the next chapter are some answers to the perennial question, "Is this the right time to invest in a mutual fund?"

8. When to Invest in a Fund

Should you wait to invest?—What are defensive and offensive stocks?
—Protection against rising living costs—"I retired on $150 a month—
and went back to work"—A recommended reading list which will
help you select a fund—How to check mutual fund market performance—Using formula plans in investing—Advantages of making
friends with your investment dealer and your mutual fund sponsor.

If you were a professional investor with over a million dollars to put to work every day earning money for you, as many
insurance companies do, your problem would not be when
to buy securities, but how to find the vast amounts of them
which would give your policyholders the results they have been
promised. The small investor has no such problem. He can
pick and choose, and make his selection at his convenience among
such stocks or bonds as may strike his fancy, or hold cash until
he feels that it is the right time to invest.

Anyone who has had to deal with investments, for himself
or for other people, realizes the importance of deciding *when*
to buy as well as what to buy. This important problem, called
timing by professionals, can be the most difficult part of investing. Holding cash, as we shall see later in this chapter, is by no
means a solution.

So, perhaps the wise thing for the small investor to do is to
follow the practice of the professionals like the insurance com-

99

panies, the colleges, hospitals, large trust accounts, and other types of securities buyers called institutional investors and invest when the money is at hand.

If you are going to do this, you will still have the problem of buying something which seems appropriate according to the condition of business and the economic outlook at the time you make your purchase. You will have to decide between *defensive* and *offensive* securities. In the first class one might put tobacco and food stocks, and in the second class what the professionals call *cyclical* stocks, that is, those which are highly regarded when business is booming but are poor earners and dividend payers when things are not so good. "Prince or pauper" industries, they are nicknamed. Most steel stocks are examples of this type.

Defense or offense in a securities portfolio can be just as important as on the gridiron, but there again the investor who buys a mutual fund is spared the making of decisions and the detail of carrying them out.

When you buy General Motors stock you make the officers and directors of that great corporation your counsel as to what should be done in the automotive field—what mechanical improvements should be included in the next year's cars, what streamlining of models might be accomplished, and how the financing of a purchase could be made easier for the buyer of a car—without any advice on your part. If you went to a bank and started a trust account you would hardly want to say to a meeting of the institution's trust officers, "Look, fellows, maybe we better not buy anything at all right now."

The same thing applies with equal force to the purchase of investment counsel whether you get it custom-made or in the convenient, ready-to-use package called the mutual fund.

Do fund managers ever make mistakes? Of course they do. Their operations may be based on what our military friends call calculated risks, but because of their training and experience they are able to spot an error of judgment and make a profitable correction of it much more readily than the private investor. Results are not guaranteed, but any reasonably complete study of mutual fund performance will tell its own story.

Since this book was first published there has been increasing interest in "growth stocks". On Page 21 are two definitions of them. If you have been doing your own investing you may have bought, or been looking at, this type of security. If so, your broker or dealer has probably mystified you (at first, anyway) by using the term "plowback". Plowback is a very important part of the growth stock formula. Why this is, and how it worked during 1953-1956, is told by a bulletin from Diversified Growth Stock Fund reading in part as follows:

Future programming is a must for companies engaged in such swiftly-changing and complex fields as atomic energy, electronics, drugs, chemicals, nucleonics, natural gas and petroleum. To help provide for expansion, most of these corporations retain a high percentage of earnings to invest in the future—even if current dividends are held to a minimum.

Such retention of earnings is called "plowback". Certain companies, of course, plow back a greater percentage of earnings than others. Among these are companies which are growing at a faster rate than industry in general. Common stocks of such companies can usually produce better than average results over the years, even though there may be substantial market swings in the interim—and even though such "growth stocks" may sometimes move counter to the general market—both up and down.

PERCENTAGE OF EARNINGS PLOWED BACK

	Dow-Jones Companies	All Mf'g Companies	46 Growth Companies
1953	40.8%	50.7%	70.1%
1954	38.5	47.1	70.1
1955	39.7	54.9	68.4
1956	31.0	54.5	67.9
Average	37.5%	51.8%	69.1%

The table at the bottom of Page 101 is reproduced from the bulletin referred to above it. Figures for "All Manufacturing Companies" are those of the Federal Trade Commission. The 46 growth companies are those in which shares were owned by Diversified Growth Stock Fund. The bulletin goes on to show comparisons of sales and profits made over the same period of years, and under the same economic conditions, by the manufacturing companies and by the growth stock companies.

In sales, the former increased 15% and the latter 44%. In profits, the manufacturing companies registered an increase of 43% while the growth stock companies gained 78%.

Mutual funds which hold stocks in their portfolios offer you protection against inflation, which is another way of saying that they are designed to help you combat rising living costs.

An old adage runs something like this: "Bees save honey, men save money, but bees do better." If you stop to think why this is true, you will realize that the value of money in itself is nothing. It is valuable only in that it can be exchanged for *things*. It is things, not money, which you eat, wear, and use.

We are indebted to Incorporated Investors for the following story about "How I Retired for Life on an Income of $150 a Month—And Went Back to Work Ten Years Later." Here is the experience of a man who had built up an estate (no matter how) which gave him an income of $150 each month, for as long as he should live.

There is nothing magic about a set income. $150 a month looked pretty good in 1939 to a lot of people. $300 a month would look pretty good to them today. The real question is, what will $300 a month buy ten, fifteen or twenty years from today. A guaranteed income always looks as safe as a church at the time you start your program. It is only as safe as the cost of living makes it.

There have been periods when a guaranteed income was the most wonderful thing in the world. Take for example the man who retired on a guaranteed income of $150 a month in 1929. Assume he was then 55 years old. Between 1929 and 1939, living costs in general declined. This man must have said to himself what a wonderful investment I made. But commencing in 1939 living costs started to rise. By 1944 this man would really start to feel the pinch. He would then be 70 years old. Having been retired for 15 years, he would have little prospect of getting a good job. Probably his only alternative would be to live out his remaining years in straightened circumstances.

The next ten years may see a decline in the cost of living, although many of the signs point the other way. But even if living costs should decline, who will guarantee there will be no further inflation over the next fifteen, twenty or thirty years? A guaranteed income may seem very safe, but if you hope for another 20 or 30 years of life, are you willing to gamble the security of your future years on that one medium of investment?

Unfortunately only a small percentage of our population took advantage of the hedge against inflation offered by mutual funds before World War II. Those who did, in most cases, found that the increase in the value of their investment and the increase in dividend income helped in a large measure to offset the inroads of rising costs. This same chance exists today, and more and more Americans are taking advantage of it.

Mutual funds cannot guarantee income—they cannot guarantee results. The values of their shares rise and fall with the performance and prospects of American industry. The dividends paid vary with the dividends received from the companies in which the funds have ownership. They are long-term investments designed to give you the kind of protection you cannot obtain from guaranteed income investments.

The objective of fund management is to increase the value of your investment and the size of your dividends over a long-term period. You know there may be times when dividends and investment value may move in opposite directions to the cost of living. You know there will be times when, for a period of years, a guaranteed income investment may be superior to an investment in a fund. Nevertheless, unless you want to gamble on a dollar that will continue stable for the rest of your life, you should consider hedging your position with shares of a recognized mutual fund.

Here is an actual example of how ownership of a fund would have protected the shareholder's purchasing power had he owned Dividend Shares from 1939 through 1957. The amount of goods (things) an individual could purchase for each $1,000 of income he received has declined over the past 19 years. This decline in purchasing power is reflected in the rising index of the cost of living prepared by the United States Bureau of Labor Statistics.

There is no sure-fire protection against inflation, but study the figures in Table 10. From time to time, the dividend income took a course contrary to that of the cost of living index, which showed a steady upward trend. Similar discrepancies may take place in the future. Any securities portfolio is subject to risks of market and income fluctuation which are moderated, though not eliminated, by broad diversification.

Table 10 shows the rise in dividends from net investment income only, assuming ownership of shares producing $1,000 in dividends in 1939. Figures are also given in terms of purchasing power by adjustment to changes in the cost of living index over the past 19 years. This record is not to be taken as an indication of future results, which may be more or less favorable. It does not include any of the capital gains distributions which were made by Dividend Shares, in varying amounts, in each of the 19 years.

Many readers may not be concerned about rising living costs. "We'll muddle through, somehow," they may feel. But something should be said here about parents looking forward to college years for their children. The future, and rising costs of education, may bring them a vital problem.

In 1900 a boy could have attended Harvard for $350, of which $150 was tuition. In 1940 the cost was $1,200, of which $400 was tuition. In 1957 the cost of the college year came to $2,150, with tuition representing $1,000. The higher figure for each year does not include anything but bare necessities. How much any child's education will cost per year depends largely on the individual case.

Other educational costs have increased in proportion to those given for Harvard University. Planning early for your child's

TABLE 10.

| | | | PURCHASING POWER | |
Year	Actual Dividends	Cost of Living Index	Dividends Received	$1,000 Annual Income
1939	$1,000	59.4	$1,000	$1,000
1940	1,679	59.9	1,666	922
1941	2,183	62.9	2,061	944
1942	2,252	69.7	1,919	852
1943	2,110	74.0	1,694	803
1944	2,061	75.2	1,628	790
1945	1,976	76.9	1,525	772
1946	1,915	83.4	1,363	712
1947	2,317	95.5	1,441	622
1948	2,520	102.8	1,457	578
1949	2,988	101.8	1,742	583
1950	3,455	102.8	1,997	578
1951	3,801	111.0	2,034	535
1952	3,496	113.5	1,828	523
1953	3,431	114.4	1,782	519
1954	3,252	114.8	1,683	517
1955	3,415	114.5	1,772	519
1956	3,659	116.2	1,871	511
1957	3,862	119.8	1,916	496

NOTE: The comparison in the above table is for a selected period, and the results shown should be considered in the light of the investment objective of Dividend Shares, the characteristics and quality of the Company's investments, and the period selected.

The record shown in this table is for a past period, and should under no circumstances be taken as an indication of future results.

college costs is prudent. In preparing for them you may wish to set aside cash savings, or buy some sort of high-grade bonds.

Suppose in 1940 you had set aside $800 for 1 year of college costs at Columbia University to be met 12 years later in 1952, only to find in 1952 that the outlay would be $1,850. Your $800 compounded over the 12 years at 2½% would have grown to $1,076. What would the difference have meant to your family budget for 1952? If a college education for your children is part of your plans, the dollar side of this problem is something that should be faced realistically.

If you would like to read a whimsical, instructive booklet dealing with the problems of rising living costs from 1935 through 1952, including the education of two children, write to Broad Street Sales Corp. at 65 Broadway, New York 6 for a copy of *The Best Laid Plans*. This is the story of Elmer, a Friendly Ghost, who observed the experiences of his wife after he had passed on, leaving her what he thought was plenty of money to take care of her and the two boys.

It seems appropriate here to mention other books which will aid you in deciding when to buy a mutual fund, and which kind seems best suited to your needs. No two volumes of this Recommended Reading are alike, and you will find in each of them certain types of material both interesting and helpful in understanding mutual funds.

High on any list of such books must be placed the annual *Manual of Investment Companies* published by Arthur Wiesenberger, head of the New York Stock Exchange firm of that name, since 1941. This is without doubt the standard reference work of the investment company industry, and covers both closed and open-end funds. Mr. Wiesenberger is a legendary figure in the investment business. After acting for several years as operating vice-president of Allied Stores, he headed the foreign department of Distributors Group, Inc., and from 1932 through 1938 handled a large volume of business with investment trusts in England, Switzerland, Scotland, and Holland.

His manual can be seen at the offices of most investment dealers and in many public libraries, or purchased direct from his firm at 61 Broadway, New York 6, for $20. It contains articles on various types of funds, the investment philosophy behind their management thinking, dollar cost averaging, the use of funds with insurance, systematic investing, and many other phases of this important form of investing. Because of its broad use it is not surprising that stories about this authoritative book have gained currency in the Street. One such deals with a young man who started his own investment firm and enjoyed a remarkably successful first year specializing in mutual funds. When a friend who knew him as a keen student of funds asked him what books had been most helpful to him, the young man replied "Arthur Wiesenberger's manual—and my Dad's check book."

Another reference work you may wish to use is the semiannual *Mutual Fund Directory* published by the *Investment Dealers' Digest* at 150 Broadway, New York 38. Price is $2 per copy. There are no sales talks in this, but it gives factual information on almost every open-end fund in the United States and many in Canada. In each case there are covered, among other facts, the size of the fund on the previous June 30 or December 31, location of its head office, the percentage of cash held, names of all officers and directors, the management organization and its fee, the sales charge, a table of distributions paid in previous years, dividend reinvestment privileges, details of its systematic investment plan if any, its liquidating provision, names of its auditors, transfer agent, and custodian, and the states in which shares are qualified for sale.

If you have been interested in reading about the results of investing in stocks, you will find additional thoughts in a book called *Common Stocks as Long Term Investments* by Edgar L. Smith, published by The Macmillan Company. This goes back many years, and developed from a study made by the author, the purpose of which was to show that high-grade bonds were better investments than stocks. Mr. Smith states in his foreword that he failed to prove this. Periods covered in the study range from 1866 to 1924. Arbitrary selections of stocks were made to avoid favoritism due to hindsight. Charts and tables illustrate the performance of stocks and bonds for various periods with regard to income, market gains, and income expressed in terms of purchasing power. Note that the span of years used covers the post bellum period in which the dollar was constantly *increasing* in purchasing power. If you want an opinion contrary to Mr. Smith's findings, read *The Common Stock Theory of Investment* by C. C. Bosland, published in 1937 by Ronald Press.

Those who wish to study modern mutual funds from the standpoint of performance will find a valuable tool in the annual edition of *Johnson's Investment Company Charts*. Hugh A. Johnson, the creator and publisher of these charts, was for many years a retailer of all types of securities in Buffalo, New York. When he became interested in mutual funds for his clients he felt the need for some authentic yardstick of performance, and his *Chart Book* was the result.

The book is now a standard piece of literature in the office of almost every dealer interested in distributing funds, and is also owned by many libraries. Mr. Johnson takes each important fund and devotes a full page in his loose-leaf book to its record for the preceding 10 years. On the page is shown the asset value at starting date, the record of an investment of $10,000 for the 10 years including the sales charge, and the results at the end of the period, including capital gains distributions. Dividends from investment income are indicated separately, as required by regulations covering all types of such material.

The book costs $35. Rand Building, Buffalo 3, is the address. For the years covered it will show you which funds rose most in value and which declined least, as well as giving you a great deal of other information about them. To compare the performances of the funds with other things, Mr. Johnson furnishes transparent overlays which you can put on top of the page representing the fund you are studying, and see how it did compared with, for instance, one of the representative stock indices, the cost of living, or even General Motors or American Tel & Tel.

In the book you now hold you will find no performance comparisons. One reason is that you should not try to compare apples and oranges, or any two unlike things. Fund records must be studied in the light of their objectives, and for comparison should be grouped together, that is, balanced funds with balanced funds, stock funds with stock funds, and so on. Even then you may be unfair to one fund or another. A second reason is that, in any book of this kind, such tables are quickly out of date. If you feel you must compare performances, here is a simple way to do it. Take the asset value per share of any fund on the date you want to start your comparison (A, below). Then take the asset value at the end of the period you wish to cover (B, below). Add to B any capital gains distributions (C, below) which have been paid during the period, and divide the sum of B and C by A.

> A was asset value of $10
> B was asset value of $11
> Add to B, C($2) $13

This would give you a sum of $13, which divided by $10 shows the asset value per share as 130% of $10 at the end of the period you used. The 100 represents 100% of your earlier asset value, leaving you with a 30% profit.

Had the fund gone off $3 in asset value during your study, your example would look like this:

> A was asset value of $10
> B was asset value of $7
> Add to B, C($2) $9

Divide $10 into $9 and you find you have 90% of your original asset value, so you know the net decline amounted to 10%.

For those who wish to delve more deeply into the subject of investment companies in general, an excellent book is *The Investment Company and the Investor,* by Rudolph L. Weissman, published by Harper & Brothers (49 East 33 St., New York 16). This is a scholarly and comprehensive work, and covers the field extremely well from a factual standpoint. Mr. Weissman, author of other books on Wall Street and on investing, is associated with W. E. Hutton & Co. of New York. He discusses in detail the policies followed and the results achieved by both closed and open-end companies.

One more book completes our Recommended Reading list. It is *Practical Formulas for Successful Investing,* by Lucile Tomlinson, published by Wilfred Funk, Inc., (33 West 46 St., New York 36). Miss Tomlinson (in private life Mrs. Alfred C. Wessmann) was formerly an associate editor of *Barron's* financial weekly, and for the last 9 years has been managing editor of Arthur Wiesenberger's annual investment company manual. In addition, she has acted as guest editor for an *Investment Dealers' Digest* supplement following each of the national mutual fund conventions held since 1949, reporting the speeches, panel discussions, and other convention events.

Many parts of her book can be read with interest and benefit by anyone wanting to know more about mutual funds, and about investing in general, but the actual formula usages she features are for the professional institutional investor of substantial means rather than the average person. Practicing what she preaches, Miss Tomlinson is accumulating money to put her daughter through college, and for that purpose uses a dollar cost averaging plan in purchasing shares of a mutual fund.

Not to skip too lightly over the subject of formula investing, it should be said that *formula plans* are devices for overcoming the frailties of human nature. Most of us are apt to go with the crowd. We buy when everybody is bullish, that is, enthusiastic about stocks and the business outlook, and we sell when everyone is bearish, or pessimistic. Incidentally, the reason times of rising securities prices are called *bull markets* is that when a bull fights he lowers his head and tries to toss his opponent into the air. Declining prices get their nickname of *bear markets* from the fact that a bear, when opposed, towers above his foe, seizes him in his huge arms, and tries to force him down by sheer weight.

Formula plans furnish what might be thought of as a financial thermostat created to indicate what an investor or an investment committee should do at certain market levels instead of going with the crowd. They first attracted considerable public notice about 20 years ago when publicity was given to the fact that both Yale University and Vassar College had put such plans into operation in connection with their investment accounts.

The general idea of using a formula plan is this: you do not know what security prices are going to do, but you are determined not to go from one emotional extreme to the other in your buying and selling. You will never go all at once from a position of full investment to one where you hold only cash, so you must set up a guide to be your financial thermostat. If you are a conservative soul whose chief objective is preservation of your capital, you will set your thermostat low as far as chances of market profits are concerned. If you are willing to take the risk the profit hunter chances, you will set it higher.

You see in this connection Chart 2 of the Dow Jones Industrial Average from 1934 through 1957. On it are channels marked with numbers from 1 to 7. Number 4 is the channel in which things are normal as far as your particular plan is concerned. For the purpose of this simple illustration, let us consider all common stocks as the aggressive (offensive) part of your investment account, and good-grade bonds as the defensive part. In Channel 4 you would be, say 50% in stocks and 50% in bonds if you are the average person wanting the benefits of formula planning but neither ultraconservative nor overspeculative. The ultraconservative investor would be 40% or

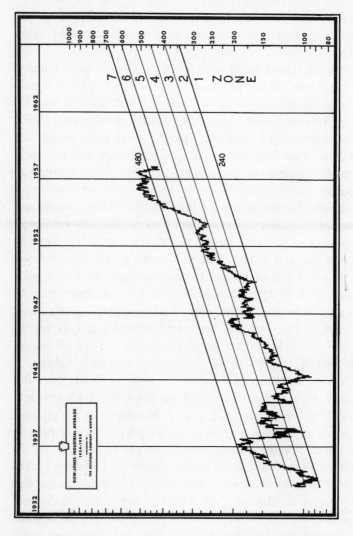

Chart 2

DOW-JONES INDUSTRIAL AVERAGE
1934-1958
PREPARED BY
THE KEYSTONE COMPANY OF BOSTON

perhaps even less in stocks in Channel 4, while the speculative-minded person would have 60% or more of his money in that aggressive section.

As the market goes higher, you would cut down your stock position and add to your bond holdings. Should the market decline, you would increase the percentage of your investment in stocks, using for this purpose the money from the bonds you sold. The reason for the seven zones is to guide formula plan investors, as such plans are usually worked out in percentages of aggressive and defensive securities to be held as the market reaches each zone.

For readers who wish to make a more complete study of formula investing we would recommend Miss Tomlinson's book, or material prepared on that subject by Keystone Custodian Funds at 50 Congress Street, Boston 9, through whose courtesy the chart is furnished, and which has long pioneered in formula planning work.

You can purchase either an aggressive or a defensive section ready-made by using shares in a mutual fund. Typical as low-cost choices for your defensive section are Series B-1 of Keystone Custodian Funds, which at this writing is 50% in United States government bonds; The Bond Fund of Boston, which is sponsored by Vance, Sanders & Company; or Institutional Bond Fund, handled by Distributors Group, Inc. These are all packages of investment quality bonds. Typical aggressive stock packages include Keystone's Series S-4 (Low-Priced Stocks), or Group Securities Capital Growth Fund.

Formula plans are not substitutes for investment management. They have nothing to do with the actual selection of the securities. Fundamentally they are protective devices. If you want to try one, do so with these ideas in mind. First, it will not make you rich but it will save you from overoptimism or the reverse. Second, to make it worth your while to try this system you must stick to your plan long enough to give it a fair chance. Third, remember that you must weigh the costs of any changes you make against their value to you.

They tell a story about a director newly elected to the board of a large financial institution who attended a meeting of the management committee and heard a discussion centering around the difficulty of avoiding shrinkage in stock accounts during periods of market decline. The new director paid close attention to what was said, and at a pause in the discussion he spoke up.

"Gentlemen," he said, "I have the solution. I move we amend our bylaws to read that we materially reduce our stock position exactly 10 days before every market decline."

No formula plan could do that, but many important institutions use such plans as counterweights against the results of becoming overbullish or overbearish. For this purpose, much is to be said in their favor.

One excellent time to buy a mutual fund is when you are satisfied by your salesman or dealer as to the experience, ability, and integrity of its management. Fund management is a profession to which many leaders of the financial fraternity have devoted their best years. In December 1953 Walter L. Morgan completed his 25th year as president of Wellington Fund. Other long-term executives in what might be called this "Quarter-Century Club" at that time included Merrill Griswold, later Chairman of the Advisory Committee of Massachusetts Investors Trust, Paul C. Cabot of State Street Investment Corporation, Hugh Bullock of the firm of Calvin Bullock, and William A. Parker, Board Chairman of Incorporated Investors. Others would include fund presidents Hugh W. Long of Fundamental Investors, S. L. Sholley of Keystone Custodian Funds, Edward C. Johnson 2nd, Fidelity Fund, Mr. and Mrs. E. W. Axe of the Axe-Houghton Funds, Henry T. Vance of Boston Fund, Francis F. Randolph, head of three mutual funds and of Tri-Continental Corporation, S. Waldo Coleman of Commonwealth Investment Company and Charles F. Eaton, Jr. of both Eaton & Howard Stock Fund and its Balanced Fund.

If you cannot meet the top executives of the funds in person, you can talk with dealers and salesmen who know them and who are familiar with their investment thinking. Make a friend of your mutual fund salesman, and confide your financial hopes and plans to him as you would other matters to your doctor or your attorney. He knows that he cannot succeed unless you do, and that no sale is a good sale unless you, the ultimate consumer, are satisfied with your purchase. Some people believe a good salesman is a fellow who can make his wife feel sorry for the poor girl who lost her hairpins in his car, but a better definition is probably "a fellow who sells goods that don't come back to customers that do."

In opening the New York Institute of Finance course on Mutual Funds in 1949 Albert P. Squier, head of the Institute, summarized the sales attitude in this way:

We hope that this course will help you place in the hands of a vast new army of investors shares in portfolios of securities whose records will bring credit to Wall Street and to the whole investment business. Those of us who have made and plan to make the investment business a long-term career are interested in a sale long after it is closed. If this fast-growing segment of the investment business is to succeed long-term, we must be ever watchful of the product that is sold.

As a mutual fund shareholder, you will be invited each year to the annual meeting. Attend if you can, by all means. You may expect to see a group of people sitting around looking wise as a tree full of owls, and you probably will. But they are human, too. After the meeting they will be glad to discuss informally with you any phase of your fund ownership you wish to mention. If you cannot meet the fund executives and managers in person, you can check them through your local bank, or find their business histories in their prospectuses and other literature. From the greenest cub salesman to the top man in the largest fund, you will find that your interests are theirs.

9. These Are Not Mutual Funds

Investment clubs can be fun, and profitable to their members—How they are formed and operated—What about the portfolios of "common trusts" in banks?—Investing in insurance stocks—Facts on the New York Stock Exchange Monthly Investment Plan—Diversification illustrated—Helpful publications to read.

A year or two ago, a New York City policeman walked into the office of *Investor* magazine. He had read an article somewhere about investment clubs and wanted to know how he and his fellow officers could supplement their retirement pensions by owning securities.

Similarly, people from all walks of life have become interested in the investment club idea, some as a means of widening their social activities, some to make money, and others for just plain fun. This "do it yourself" investing has captured the imagination of thousands of the American public and helped them learn basic investment principles.

The idea started in Michigan and was fathered largely by George A. Nicholson, Jr. of the Detroit firm of Watling, Lerchen & Co. These clubs, of which there were more than 8,000 in early 1958, have their national association and publish a monthly bulletin called the *News,* carrying data about club activities and educational material on methods of investing and club operation. At their third national convention, held in Detroit in October 1953, they were addressed by Edward T.

McCormick, President of the American Stock Exchange, who told the delegates:

> It seems to me that you, and not Wall Street, have found a practical answer to selling shares in our future. Investment clubs have found a realistic way to enable the small investor to purchase common stock and to participate in an important manner in the maintenance and growth of our economic system. The clubs are spreading the gospel of stock ownership at a level where such gospel is meaningful and effective.

Another active sponsor of investment clubs is *Investor* magazine itself. Information about such clubs, and sample sets of bylaws, can be had by writing its Federation of Investment Clubs, 150 Broadway, New York 38.

An investment club is a group of friends or acquaintances who join together and usually contribute some fixed number of dollars each month, which is invested for them as a group. There are no membership dues or fees of any kind. Most clubs are made up of members who meet in a home or office once a month, make their deposits, and decide what security shall be their next purchase. Usually a club starts because one interested person wants to try out the idea and persuades his friends to join him. Together they select others until they have a group of 12 or more. For practical operation, 40 seems to be about the top number of members.

When the group has been formed it holds a meeting, discusses a general plan for its future, and draws up its bylaws. When this has been done, and officers elected, the club is ready to start its activities. Unless some member is qualified to do so, it is well to have present at the first meeting someone familiar with securities to discuss them, as well as the routine of purchases and sales. Usually some registered representative of a stock exchange firm will be glad to attend, or your local investment dealer can help you. If no such person is available, write to the National Association of Investment Clubs, 2232 National

Bank Building, Detroit 26, or to the Federation of Investment Clubs mentioned above.

Probably the investment man you have invited to your meeting will talk to you about the importance of sticking to your plan once it is started. He will also point out some of the pitfalls of investing, and some fundamentals in the selection of securities. He will also probably caution your members against expecting profits too large, or too soon.

If he is to be present only at your first meeting he can help you by suggesting a series of questions you may wish to ask about possible candidates for your future investments. Generally a club buys one stock a month. Individual members are assigned the duty of studying various industries and the companies in them. At following meetings, they report their choice or choices, and when a selection has been agreed upon, the order is placed through the dealer or broker you want to use.

No greatly detailed bookkeeping setup is necessary. One of your members is appointed as agent by the others, and authorized to place your buying and selling orders. Your dealer or broker holds the securities you own in the name of the club (*not* the name of your agent) and collects dividends for you. To avoid the bookkeeping of distributing small dividends at the start, most clubs tell the dealer or broker to reinvest them, thus adding to the value of the share of each club member as time goes on.

Your bookkeeper will want to keep a record of the name of each member, what and when he has contributed, number of shares he owned each month, asset value per share each month, securities purchased with date and price, securities sold, dividends received, and club expenses.

New members can be taken into your club by selling them shares at asset value, which you saw how to figure in Chapter 1, where we divided the total value of the home-made mutual fund by the number of shares it had out. On the same basis, investment club members may buy additional shares each month.

The tax status of unincorporated investment clubs is uncertain at this writing. The Internal Revenue Service, when questioned, has stated that the frequently-used joint syndicate arrangement is, for tax purposes, a corporation. Evidently a straightforward partnership arrangement is accepted as such by the tax authorities.

If there is a disagreement about your "stock of the month," those who do not want to accept the temporary investment committee's choice may forego investing in that issue. It is because of this possibility that those who have run successful investment clubs urge that the memberships be kept small. Most of the fun and interest in these clubs comes through having a rotating investment committee, which usually consists of two different members each month. They are charged with the responsibility, either on their own or with the assistance of your investment advisor, of examining investments, analyzing their good and bad points, and making recommendations to the next meeting.

It is a good idea to keep your club investments small—about $10 a month from each member seems to be about the best sum. Short-term trading operations should be avoided, and you will find that clubs looking for "quick turns" in the market seldom last long. Individuals may perhaps be able to trade successfully, but few clubs have done so.

One of the earliest of such clubs was started in 1940 when six ambitious young Detroiters got out of college. Their objective was to get together enough money to start a business in which they would all be partners. World War II and other considerations have kept this goal something yet to be attained, but a total of about $17,000 has been put to work over the years. Some $10,000 has been withdrawn, but in late 1953 this particular club had assets worth $44,000.

Probably as you have been reading you have asked yourself, "What has this to do with mutual funds?" Actually, very little. The sole resemblance is that a group of people join together for mutual benefit in investing. Except in rare cases they lack the professional first selection of their stocks and bonds. They lack entirely the advantage of wide enough diversification to give them a real spreading of risk. They are at a tremendous disadvantage in spotting bad situations which indicate that a holding should be sold. Unless they buy the same stock every month for a long time (which would defeat both the "fun" and the educational purposes of the club) they cannot benefit from dollar cost averaging.

However, some of the investment clubs confine their purchases to shares in mutual funds, preferring to let professional managers do their selecting and supervising for them. Other clubs put part of their money into funds, and part into what they believe are growth situations. Or, like some shrewd investors of substantial means, they use shares in mutual funds to salt away market profits which they regard as a financial reserve.

Leaving investment clubs to their almost limitless future, let us look at two types of professionally managed portfolios which are sometimes confused with mutual funds. One is what banks and trust companies call *common trusts*. The other is insurance stocks.

Common trusts does not mean common stock trusts. It is a term applied by banks with trust powers to comingled accounts. In much the same way as an investment counsel firm handles small accounts by having a mutual fund in which it sells shares, these banks have set up the common trusts to take care of people whose means do not permit the opening of full-fledged trust accounts. A bank or trust department will put a number of small accounts together and make one common account, or trust, large enough so that the managers can give it reasonable diversification in its holdings—a diversification impossible with a small amount of money.

When you open one of these accounts you accept the management of the institution's security-watching service, just as you would if you invested in a mutual fund. There is this difference, however. When the *trust instrument* is drawn up (this is the legal document under which the trust is to be handled, and covers agreed-upon restrictions as to what kind of securities may be bought, what the charges will be, and so forth) the maker can specify whether or not he wants certain types of securities in the account. He may wish to confine his managers, or executors, to investments legal for trustees under the laws of the state in which the trust is to operate, or he may indicate that he wants nothing but bonds or preferred stocks to be held. He may give them entire discretion as to what to buy. He may, as many do, state that shares in mutual funds shall be a satisfactory holding for his trust account. With regard to this point, state laws vary. See your investment dealer as to the situation where you live.

Most states will accept mutual fund shares as trustee investments. In any piece of literature listing the institutional holders of a fund you will find a large percentage of trustees and trust accounts.

According to an article in *Trusts and Estates* magazine in early 1958 there were 269 common funds in operation in banks in 41 states, District of Columbia, and Hawaii. Their assets were almost $2 billion. Among other holdings they owned common stocks in 642 different corporations. The average size account participating in a common trust fund was about $22,000.

Such common trusts are subject to regulations of the Board of Governors of the Federal Reserve System. An analysis of more than 150 trust funds from their 1957 reports indicates their holdings as follows:

Government bonds	12.8%
Corporate bonds	23.5
Preferred stocks	9.8
Common stocks	52.3
All other holdings	1.6

Trust accounts are usually valued 4 times a year on the last business days of January, April, July, and October. Fees for having your money in a common trust are usually the same as if you had your personal trust. Management fees are fixed by the state in which the trust operates, and so are the charges against principal, and both are figured on an annual basis. Persons interested in this form of money management should consult a bank with trust powers as to entering costs, management and other charges, and possible termination fee, which would be stated in advance when the trust instrument is drawn up.

You read earlier in Chapter 1 how the New York State Savings Banks had formed a mutual fund (Institutional Investors Mutual Fund) for the convenience of their members in having their investments watched, or supervised. For the same reason, the New York State banks with trust powers in early 1954 were forming their own mutual fund, designed particularly to service the common trusts, which hold only "legal" investments. The public cannot buy shares in either of these funds organized by the banks, but the fact that both types of institutions have adopted the mutual fund structure and idea is a solid tribute to the convenience and results of professional investment management supplied in this handy packaged form.

Let us look now at insurance company stocks as compared with mutual funds. Some people think (and rightly) that insurance companies have some smart people looking after their investments. Big companies usually have their own analytical staffs, and smaller companies generally employ professional investment counsel. Also, there are some which get their securities management at least in part by owning mutual fund shares. For instance, a small company might consider itself capable of managing the bond portion of its portfolio (probably mostly in U. S. government obligations) but would cover its need for stock investment by owning shares in a mutual fund in that field.

Insurance companies are primarily in the insurance business, not the business of investing money. The valuation the public places on their stocks in the market place represents what the public thinks of their ability to combine successfully a profitable insurance business (underwriting) with an investment account. In the public mind, the underwriting comes first, and public estimates of the value of insurance company shares take little account of gains or losses in the value of their investments.

Underwriting has been a profitable business most of the time, but in some years there have been substantial losses. A mutual fund is not subject to underwriting risks. Insurance companies pay dividends only from investment income, and keep all the underwriting earnings. The mutual fund pays shareholders both its investment income and its realized profits, or capital gains. The shareholder in an insurance company has no direct benefit from a rise in the market value of its investments. A mutual fund shareholder does benefit. Market prices of insurance stocks change with public opinion and are subject to supply and demand as well as business conditions. Mutual fund shares can be offered for redemption at asset value on any business day.

So much for insurance stocks. Now, let us look at a plan which may have made January 25, 1954 a red letter day in the history of the New York Stock Exchange. On that date it became possible for an investor to purchase shares of listed stocks by paying as little as $40 a month or every three months. Officially known as MIP (the Monthly Investment Plan), it was launched by G. Keith Funston, president of the Exchange, after months of careful preparation and study.

Here is the thinking behind the plan, as summarized by Mr. Funston:

A nation of share owners is our strongest defense against the foreign "isms" that would sap our vitality and eventually turn us over to the evil enemy we know as communism. We can preach the virtues of capitalism until we are blue in the face, but one stock certificate in the name of Joe Public is a stronger argument than all the oratory of which we are capable.

Public ownership of the means of production is perhaps the only way by which we can insure the proper functioning of an enlightened capitalistic society. The basic characteristic of capitalism is that thrifty people can put their surplus funds to work in the ownership of industry, and may participate in the profits. There is no Stock Exchange in Moscow, nor is ownership in promising enterprises in Russia available to the public.

On the first day MIP was available, 283 orders were placed with 55 member firms of the Exchange. They represented investment in 658 shares of 142 different stocks to a market value of $21,333. Up to the end of 1957 the 65,000 plans then outstanding, plus those completed or terminated, had accounted for the purchase of about 2,000,000 shares of stock with a market value of some $75,000,000. About 88% of MIP owners were reinvesting their dividends to accumulate money more quickly. Those who invest quarterly slightly outnumbered those who make payments each month. Here is a list showing the ten "most popular" stocks when MIP started in January 1954 and the leading ten in late 1957. Early in 1958, Tri-Continental and Sperry Rand changed places.

1954	*1957*
Radio Corporation	General Electric
American Tel. & Tel.	General Motors
General Motors	Dow Chemical
Dow Chemical	Standard Oil (N.J.)
Standard Oil (N.J.)	Sperry Rand
United States Steel	Radio Corporation
Tri-Continental Corp.	Tri-Continental Corp.
Long Island Lighting	American Tel. & Tel.
duPont	Phillips Petroleum
Socony-Vacuum Oil	American Airlines

Editor Kenneth Hayes of the New York Stock Exchange monthly magazine *Exchange* in writing about MIP, said,

All legends die hard, but not many have clung as tenaciously to life as the ancient myth that ownership of listed common stocks is confined largely to the wealthy few.

Actually, of course, that bit of folklore took a pretty severe drubbing when the Brookings Institution disclosed (in its 1952 survey) that 1,220,000 of the 6,500,000 individuals in this country who held stocks of publicly owned corporations were members of family groups with annual incomes of less than $4,000.

In the light of this, it is evident that there is a broad market for MIP and similar plans. The MIP is a method of purchasing stocks by the dollar's worth, just as the modern gasoline pump makes it possible to buy $1 or $5 worth of gas whether the price is 29½ or 31¼ cents a gallon. It is definitely not a get-rich-quick scheme. The only risks assumed are those of anyone owning property. The price of your shares bought under the plan may go up or down depending on earnings, prospects, and the state of business generally. The risk is the same as if you owned 100 or 1,000 shares of the same stock or, for that matter, a house. Here is how MIP works:

Basically, it is an extension of the idea which has enabled millions of Americans in medium- and low-income groups to pay out of income for their homes, automobiles, and household appliances. It does not involve the use of credit, but does allow the person of moderate means to buy a share of industry by small periodic payments.

The regular New York Stock Exchange commissions are charged. These are 6% on amounts up to $100 and $3 plus 1% (but not less than $6 on any single purchase) for larger amounts. The buyer indicates his or her intention to invest certain amounts of money over a certain period, but there is no penalty for giving up a plan. Dividends on stocks owned may be left to be reinvested in more shares or will be mailed to the owner, as he directs. At the end of the agreed period of investment a certificate for the shares he has bought will be

You Stock Exchange fellows certainly get around.

mailed to him, and if any fractional shares are owned they can be sold for cash.

Included in the cost of each purchase you make, unless it should happen to be 100 shares or a multiple of 100, will be what is called an *odd-lot* charge. An odd lot is anything under 100 shares, and an odd-lot broker is a man or firm who receives a small fee for breaking up 100-share certificates of the stock you want into smaller amounts, thus making it possible for you to buy one, or nine, or any number of shares under 100. On stocks selling under $40 this odd-lot charge is 12½c per share; above $40 it is 25c per share. This charge you pay in addition to your brokerage commission, for the convenience of buying small amounts of shares.

Here is the illustration used by the New York Stock Exchange as a sample of how to start an MIP:

Mr. Jones decides to invest $40 a month in a stock selling at $29⅞ a share. His first month's order is executed on the Exchange at the odd-lot price of $30. After provision of $2.26 for the 6% commission on the investment of the $37.74 balance, he immediately becomes the owner of one full share and $7.74 worth of a second share—a total of 1.258 shares. The following month (assuming the price has not changed) he will own two full shares (costing $60) plus $15.48 worth of a third share—a total of 2.516 shares.

Nobody can do more than estimate for you what your in-and-out cost would be if you complete your plan, or if you discontinue it. The reason for this is that your "getting-out" cost would vary widely according to the price of the stock you were in, and the amount of money involved. Here is a fair presentation of the matter by long-time top-flight financial writer Burton Crane, who in *The New York Times* of December 20, 1953 covered MIP in a feature story and compared its costs with those of buying mutual funds:

Comparisons between MIP and mutual funds are not easy. If a man paid in $100 under MIP and then sold out he would lose more than 12% in commissions and odd-lot differentials. Sales costs on mutual funds range from 7¼ to 9¼%, all on the buy side. There is no charge for selling out.

Suppose, however, that the investor under MIP paid in his $40 a month for a year and a half. If the shares remained in the 19 to 20 price range he would have paid about $4.13 in odd-lot differentials and about $40.68 in commissions and would own about $675 worth of stock. The cost would have been about 6.22%.

When he sold his thirty-three and a fraction shares, however, he would come into a new commission band. The total selling cost, including odd-lot differential, would be $13.73 so that his complete round trip would have cost him $58.54 or 8.13%, about midway in the mutual fund scale.

Nobody, however, should compare the purchase of a mutual fund with MIP. Each has its own purpose and value. Granting that an intelligent broker can suggest an attractive stock to be purchased through MIP, the professional investment management available through mutual funds can also do so, and such a purchase will give diversification as well.

On this matter of diversification in mutual fund portfolios an actual illustration may be in order. Let us pick up the annual report (for the calendar year 1957) issued by Fidelity Fund, which on December 31 showed assets of $232,089,331 and had outstanding 19,799,596 shares owned by 66,300 investors of all types from individuals to large institutions. Fidelity's portfolio was divided like this: 85.5% was in common stocks, 2.0% in preferred stocks, 11.4% in bonds (including obligations of the United States) and the remaining 1.1% in cash. There were 191 issues of securities, representing more than 30 major industries.

Suppose you had owned $10,000 worth of Fidelity Fund on December 31, 1957. To many this sounds like a fortune, and we might suppose that a large part of our investment would be in one, or maybe in one or two companies.

Actually, the largest portions of your $10,000 investment

(exclusive of U. S. obligations) would have been $299 in Cities Service, $275 in Bethlehem Steel, $249 in International Paper, $223 in U. S. Steel and $212 in International Business Machines. In no other issue was more than $200 of your money represented. There were 13 issues in each of which you would have had between $100 and $200. Of the other 173 issues held, 60 would each have represented between $50 and $100 of your capital, and 113 less than $50, running down to 1 at $5 and 1 at only $4.

That is typical of the diversification you get in a mutual fund. Moreover, you have a "built-in" watching service for your securities, a service which will look ahead and make needed changes for you with no inconvenience on your part. You get a full-time job based on ability and experience.

Some of the means by which information about portfolio securities is gathered are of interest. In its stone castle at Tarrytown-on-the-Hudson, E. W. Axe & Co. keep up to date more than 2,000 charts from which trained investment officers are able to get long-range views of a particular corporation or industry, or of economic trends. Investors Diversified Services of Minneapolis, which manages Investors Mutual, a fund which on December 31, 1957, had almost a billion dollars in assets, is visited almost daily by senior executives of companies whose securities they own. More often than not, these executives bring with them their own economists to discuss with the I.D.S. management their viewpoints pertaining to their own companies and industries.

A unique feature of the offerings of Vance, Sanders & Company is that their investment companies benefit from diversification of management, three separate and distinct supervisory organizations being responsible for the management of their six funds. One is concerned with Century Shares Trust, another with Boston Fund, Canada General Fund, and The Bond Fund of Boston, and the third with Massachusetts Investors Trust and with Massachusetts Investors Growth Stock Fund.

National Securities & Research Corporation covers broad fields of finance and economics, and its annual forecast is widely read among the investment fraternity, some 300,000 copies being distributed each year to banks, executives, and other centers of financial information. All the material gathered is used first, of course, in the interests of the organization's various fund portfolios.

Another widely known publication is *Brevits,* issued by Vance, Sanders & Company in the interest of its distributors, who often pass along copies to investors. In *Brevits*, Editor Edward E. Hale features financial and economic data of a factual nature, helpful to anyone interested in or concerned with the ownership or management of securities.

Also well known in that field are *Perspective,* published by Calvin Bullock, Ltd., and the Annual Forecasts issued by Selected American Shares. *Perspective* is largely on the statistical side and is widely read by economists and by bank and insurance officials, as well as investment dealers. Selected American's Forecasts, and its other material for dealers and investors, are written largely by president Edward P. Rubin, who has a rare knack of "unscrewing the inscrutable" by interpreting financial jargon in understandable terms.

Current information on what professional investors are doing is always of interest. The private investor can find in print quarterly surveys of what the various funds are buying and selling. Prominent among these is one copyrighted by Henry Ansbacher Long which appears in *Barron's* financial weekly. It shows the number of shares of stock in each company bought and sold during the preceding quarter by most of the important mutual funds.

Arthur Wiesenberger & Company has a similar quarterly study (Portfolio Periscope) and another, by mutual fund columnist Charles Brophy, appears in the New York *Herald-Tribune*. In the same paper, general financial columnist C. Norman Stabler at times writes on mutual funds, as does Financial Editor Donald

I. Rogers. On the West coast, San Francisco papers carry informative mutual fund items by Financial Editor John S. Piper in the *News,* Sidney P. Allen in the *Chronicle* and Lindsay Arthur in the *Call-Bulletin.*

Perhaps you feel that mutual funds are not for you. They are not—and neither should other securities be—until you first have a fair bank account and an insurance program. Perhaps you will find in the next chapter some of the reasons—in addition to "I have no money"—which you (and others) have given for not wanting to buy mutual fund shares.

10. "I Object—"

Four reasons some people are not interested in mutual funds—
Could 1929 come back?—It is fun to pick your own stocks—What
can an investor expect in results from a fund?—What about costs?
—The best suggestion about mutual funds in this book.

If you talked to a hundred people who did not want to invest
in mutual funds, you would probably find that their lack of
interest could be classified under 4 general headings:

1. They are afraid 1929 might come back.
2. They like to pick their own stocks.
3. They feel that, unlike some forms of investment which
"guarantee" a rate of interest, or the delivery of a certain number of dollars on some future date, mutual funds contain some
element of uncertainty as to whether the user will get his money
back.
4. They think it costs too much to buy a fund.

Of these, the possible return of a 1929 is certainly the $64
question. What the asker really means is probably "If a severe
business depression hit the United States and securities prices
declined, what would happen to holders of mutual funds?" Let's
shadow-box that one for a few minutes.

First, let us dispose of Uncle Willie. Sooner or later you
will meet someone who had an Uncle Willie by that name or
some other who in 1929 lost all his money in investment trusts.

There was a family on relief, and to the consternation of the county worker added to its number at an average of one about every 11 months. The worker frequently admonished Sam, the daddy of the flock, but the production line continued to function. Finally Sam was warned that with the next addition the relief checks would stop.

In due course another bundle from Heaven arrived, and Sam went into the woods to hang himself. He stood on a large box, threw a rope over a limb and knotted it around his neck. As he was about to kick the box out from under him a sudden thought crossed his mind.

"Sam," he said to himself, "don't act too quick. You might be hangin' the wrong man!"

If in some way you are confusing investment trusts as they operated in 1929 with the present-day mutual fund, and are inclined to place the blame on today's open-end companies for the losses of investors, be sure you do not "hang the wrong man."

Mutual funds have the liquidating provision through which shares can be presented for redemption on any business day. The old-time investment trusts had no such provision. The following quotation from the Securities & Exchange Commission Report to Congress on Investment Companies (1939, Part II, page 242) contains some facts about the liquidating provision in the early days:

During the period from 1927 to 1936 the 40 open-end companies (mutual funds) which constitute almost the entire group and on which most of the statistics have been based paid $142,000,000 in redeeming their own shares, or an amount equal to about 25% of the $564,000,000 of shares sold by such companies during the same period. . . . Redemptions exceeded sales in only two quarters of the 10-year period and then only by small amounts.

It is interesting that even in the 1927-1936 period, sales exceeded redemptions by 4 to 1. Sales exceeded redemptions in every year, including 1929, 1930, 1931, and 1932.

At the hearings before the Senate Banking and Currency Committee in 1940, on the bill introduced to regulate investment companies (Part II, page 496) Mr. Merrill Griswold, now Chairman of the Board of Trustees of Massachusetts Investors Trust, which in every year since it started in 1924 has registered a growth in number of shares outstanding, referred to a theory advanced by an SEC witness of a possible run on open-end companies, like a run on a bank. He testified:

An open-end company is not committed to repay a given number of dollars, as a bank is. It merely repays on demand a certain specified percentage of its assets. . . . Therefore, no open-end investment company such as ours can ever become insolvent.

Moreover, the investments of an open-end management trust, comprising a diversified list of highly marketable common stocks, are far easier to liquidate quickly . . . than are the assets of a commercial bank, savings bank or life insurance company.

There is nothing in the sixteen-year record of the open-end trusts that gives the slightest reason for the belief that "runs" on them would take place. There were no such runs in 1929 or the early 1930's during the heaviest security liquidation that ever occurred in this country. There were no such runs during the violent market decline of 1937. . . . The shares of an open-end company are not a bank deposit.

It is conceivable that all of the depositors of a bank might decide at the same time that it was wise for them to withdraw their funds. But it is inconceivable that all the holders of an open-end trust would simultaneously decide to liquidate their investments. The very market action that would cause some holders to liquidate would cause others to hold or increase their investments.

Illustrating an actual occurrence along the lines mentioned in Mr. Griswold's testimony, here is part of a talk given by Hugh Bullock, son of the founder of the firm of Calvin Bullock, which was established in 1894, at the New York Institute of Finance on March 22, 1949:

The marketability of an investment company of the open-end type should be tremendously emphasized. Talk about parity prices and government props under various commodities. Those are nothing compared to the self-liquidating feature of a good mutual fund.

Back in 1929, on some of the days that fall, there were certainly periods of acid test. One of our companies had assets of over $50,000,000. In a period of less than a week over $3,000,000 worth of its shares were thrown back at us. Those were days when the most active stock on the New York Exchange for the year 1929, Electric Bond & Share, closed without a bid. We never failed to bid for our particular shares.

There was always the safety factor of the self-liquidating feature to back us up. And any liquidation would exert only minor pressure on a broad list of securities, as against major pressure if an equal dollar volume of any specific security were pressed for liquidation on the Exchange. In short, our company's shares proved to have a better market on certain days than the then most active stock on the Exchange.

Nothing in this chapter is intended to imply that a holder of mutual fund shares can at any time liquidate them for exactly what he paid. As your dealer or salesman must tell you, the holder who liquidates may receive either less or more than his purchase price. But the liquidation provision is written into the mutual fund structure. You will find it detailed in any prospectus.

Should a period similar to 1929 come, all securities will sell off in price. Probably shares in well-managed mutual funds would not decline so much as a general hodgepodge of securities, for two reasons. First, the fund managers will to some extent at least have prepared for bad financial weather, and because of their experience they are qualified to roll with the punches when trying times are at hand. Second, their holdings are apt to be of higher investment quality than the hodgepodge list, and for that reason should act better defensively. Should all securities sell off, those owned by your bank and your insurance company will be included. Managers of such investment accounts have their problems, too.

However, this writer does not believe another 1929 is in the making. Times have changed. In 1929 there were no social security benefits, there were no guarantees by federal agencies of certain forms of bank and savings accounts. The investment counsel business as it is known today could hardly have been said to have made a start in size, experience, or availability.

Since 1929 the whole financial climate has changed. The caliber of financial news has shown vast improvement. Stock pools and manipulations have been outlawed. Stocks were boosted much higher in relation to earnings and dividends than they sell today. As you read earlier in the University of Michigan experience, common stocks have attained an investment stature which has led to vast amounts of the blue chips being taken out of the market by institutional accounts which would have looked down their noses at such investments even 15 years ago.

Another 1929 will not come along until we develop another generation of margin traders. In that era a speculator who put up as much as 10% margin ($100 for each $1,000 worth of stock he wanted to buy) was regarded as conservative. Office boys and messengers would pool their cash and speculate during their lunch hour in hopes of making a quick turn in some currently touted stock. In those easy days, in-and-out commissions amounted to about a quarter of a point, leaving as a profit anything over those expenses.

Now a 50% margin is required, brokerage commissions are higher, and the capital gains tax on a short-term trade (one where the security is held less than 6 months) will take half of your profit, should you make one. No wonder the loose money which used to go into margin trading now finds its way to the race tracks or the numbers games.

Business cycles being what they are, and human nature what it is, depressions may strike again, but 1929 conditions will not return until margins are materially lowered and until all your friends begin bragging about the wonderful market tips they have been getting, and how much they have been making trading in stocks. Watch out, when everybody claims to be like the

I can't remember the name of the stock, but the reports just fit the
bottom of Jackie's cage.

> . . . old lady from Wheeling
> Who for trading developed a feeling.
> She would buy her stocks back
> When the market would crack,
> After selling them out at the ceiling.

Probably during the first part of the next "1929" you will hear a lot from our friend who brings up Objection No. 2, "I like to pick my own stocks." More power to him. It is fun, and some few individuals seem endowed with skill, intuition, or whatever it takes to do well marketwise. When you meet such a person he has been either smart or lucky. If lucky, he will stub his toe sooner or later, like the rest of us. If smart, he has probably insured his life to protect his family, but he cannot insure that fact that he will remain with them always to supply investment advice. Is his widow-to-be thoroughly familiar with the details of selecting, diversifying, watching, and selling securities? He cannot leave his investment knowledge behind, but he can leave to her professional management and freedom from detail and worry by making the securities part of his estate a list of shares in mutual funds.

Objection No. 3, "There's no guarantee I'll get my money back," is really a question not of number of dollars but of purchasing power. One of the strongest features about mutual funds is that the result of investing in them is not limited to 2½% or 3% a year. True, it may be smaller, but if history continues its trend of the last hundred years the dollar will buy less and less, or it will take more dollars to maintain whatever standard of living the investor believes he should have. A dollar worth 100 cents in 1850 was worth 23 cents 100 years later. Even as recently as the early 1930's it was worth 35 cents in purchasing power. Mutual funds cannot guarantee you dollar amounts returned, but on the basis of their records the investor will get his money back in terms of the purchasing power of his returned dollars. This does not mean that fixed income investment should be avoided, as financial reserves are necessary. However, they are only part of a sound all-over financial plan, which should include common stocks to hedge the risk of fixed-dollar contracts.

Our friend who brings up Objection No. 4, "It costs too much to buy a fund," should consider that he is buying not a scrambled handful of stocks for which he immediately assumes full responsibility, but a finished product with built-in advantages. He probably knows that the actual materials which make up his telephone are worth only about $3, but he cheerfully pays $10 a month or more for the benefits and convenience the completed instrument gives him.

If he is thinking in terms of costs too high, he should be fair enough to relate the sales charge in a mutual fund to other profit margins. What do you suppose was the dealer's profit when he bought his last car, or his latest suit, and what portion do you suppose was retained by the company when he paid his first insurance premium? He should remember that the fund's sales charge covers both his entering and liquidating expense, and that it is there instead of brokerage commissions and other fees.

In its February 1954 issue, *Investor* magazine carried an article headed "The Mutual Fund—A Bargain Purchase." Included was a table based on a survey made by an impartial research organization (Table 12).

Louis H. Whitehead of the New York Stock Exchange firm of Cosgrove, Miller & Whitehead, who was a professor of economics at Syracuse University before coming to Wall Street, and who has both wholesaled and retailed funds as well as addressing all types of audiences on general investment matters, comments on the sales charge of a mutual fund in this way:

If the lowest dollar cost were always the criterion by which services are judged there would be no market for Cadillacs or Buicks, and General Motors would drop everything except its Chevrolet line. Both the Chevrolet and the Cadillac provide dependable transportation service. Why then do people put up about

TABLE 12.　ACQUISITION COSTS
(As percentage of retail price)

Mutual funds (approx. average)	7½
Casualty and fire insurance	20
Life insurance	50[a]
Checking accounts	15–20
Small personal loans	30
Furniture	40–60
Automobiles	33
Television sets	30
Appliances	33
Liquor	30
Books	40
Women's clothing	45
Men's shirts	40
Shoes	30

[a] Applies only to first year's premium on most types of life insurance.

twice the cost of one to buy the other? Simply this—they pay whatever is necessary to get a Cadillac because they want the things that only a Cadillac provides—superior comfort, luxurious appointments, the prestige and sense of well-being that goes with owning the car most people speak of as "biggest and best." A less expensive car will take you to your destination and bring you back just about as well as a Cadillac, but a large number of people do not hesitate to pay more for a Cadillac because its "added features" are important to them. Correspondingly there are many people who, if informed about mutual funds, would gladly discontinue fumbling around with their own investments and adopt the mutual fund idea for its "added features."

In addition to other features mentioned in these pages, the following characteristics should not be overlooked:

1. Think of a fund as a stone wall. Consider every security in the portfolio as a stone in that wall. One or two or more may deteriorate, but the wall will stand. In fact, it is the job of the

management to see that stones are replaced before the deterioration can hurt the wall. Due to the soundness of such a structure, your principal sum invested in a fund should never be destroyed.

2. Imagine a huge tank into which 80 or 100 streams of dividends are pouring. On the bottom is a tap, through which you receive your share. Some of the lines may clog but the flow from your tap will never stop, though it may slow somewhat from time to time.

3. When market declines do come, the price of your fund shares will decline, but it will not be like an individual stock, which may go down with the rest and never recover. Due to their cross-section-investment nature, plus watchful management, your shares will enjoy recovery in price with other sound securities when business again improves.

A share in a mutual fund is, in the final analysis, a share in American industry. You own its tools and factories. You help elect directors. You have an interest in everything the portfolio companies earn, and the dividends they pay. With thousands of investors across the United States you have a part in supplying the money for new products, better services, and more earning power.

An Englishman, and an American who was a substantial holder of mutual funds, were being presented at the court of a foreign potentate who received the Englishman with "We are proud to welcome a subject of your great nation."

Then, turning to the American he said, "And you, I suppose, are a subject of the United States."

"Subject, Hell," roared the American. "I *own* part of the United States."

Which fund for you?

The purpose of this book has been to guide you in finding out, but its most helpful suggestion is that you talk freely with some dealer in whom you have confidence. Let him help you select what is best suited to your needs.

Years ago, when the writer was a young salesman of securities, he was invited to address the National Industrial Research Council on "What Research Means to the Investor." Knowing nothing about the subject, but being acquainted with many investors, he thought he would prepare for his talk by finding out their opinions. Picking up his phone he called a Mr. Braunstein over in Brooklyn, who owned a small garment factory.

"Good morning, Mr. B.," says the writer. "I want to talk to you about research."

"What's that?" yelled Mr. B. over the racket of his machines.

"Research. Industrial research. I want to talk to you about it."

"Well," replied Mr. Braunstein, "I'm pretty busy this morning, and I can't hear you very well. But if you say it's all right —I'll take fifty shares!"

May you, Mr., Mrs., or Miss Reader, find a dealer in whom you have confidence, and start with him on the quest for your mutual fund and the reassurance about your investments it will bring you.

11. Recent Developments

What's new in mutual funds since 1953—Introduction of variable annuities—Using systematic withdrawal plans—More new Canadian investment companies—Proposals for municipal (tax free) bond funds—New laws on securities gifts to minors—Other facts of interest.

Various new factors have affected the mutual fund business since 1953 when this book was first written. Among these has been the introduction of legislation in New Jersey and other states which would permit insurance companies to create and sell what are termed "variable annuities." These are periodic payments based upon the values of past investments in common stocks. Their adoption was recommended by some (not all) of the insurance companies as a means by which the policy holder would find his annuity payments greater or less in amount as securities prices rose and fell, thus giving him an income adjusted to changes in living costs as inflation or deflation took hold in the American economy.

Leader in the effort to introduce variable annuities was Prudential Life Insurance Company of Newark. Chief opposition from the industry was led by Frederic W. Ecker, president of New York's Metropolitan Life. Also opposing it were the National Association of Securities Dealers, the Investment Bankers Association of America and the Securities & Exchange Commission as well as other organizations connected with the distribution of investments.

In early 1958 the matter was still in the courts. A September 1957 decision by Judge Wilkins in the District Court, District of Columbia, dismissed complaints (by the SEC and NASD) which sought to enjoin two variable annuity companies from selling their contracts until they had registered as investment companies and the contracts had been registered with SEC as securities. The court stated that it would have been constrained to find in favor of the complainants were it not for the McCarran-Ferguson Insurance Regulation Act of 1945, which gave state insurance authorities exclusive jurisdiction over organizations registered as insurance companies. The issue then reached the U. S. Court of Appeals in Washington where NASD and SEC appealed from the District Court decision but received a ruling that variable annuity contracts are not subject to SEC regulation. Final decision may come from the U. S. Supreme Court, or the matter may go to Congress.

Since 1953 (and this is no doubt one reason why the variable annuities were proposed) wide public attention has been given to the effects of inflation on purchasing power, and the difficulty of providing adequate income for the years of retirement which must be faced by people (or their widows) no longer active in business. Efforts were made by various sources to provide suitable means for making available additional income to supplement social security payments and such other monies as might be available but would not suffice for required living needs.

On page 97 is a discussion of how College Retirement Equities Fund was established. This fund is available only to members of the teaching profession. However, since 1953 many of the mutual funds have offered what are known as systematic withdrawal plans by which any investor having accumulated a certain minimum amount (usually $10,000) in a fund may have the fund (or its bank) pay him monthly or quarterly such a sum as he may desire, this sum being used by him to supplement his other income.

"Some interesting calculations can be made," Edward E. Hale

wrote in Vance, Sanders & Company's *Brevits,* "of how the regular purchase of investment company shares can be used to establish a capital sum which may be drawn upon as a source of retirement income. The principle involved is to invest regularly for a period of years and then, at some desired point, to start withdrawing money regularly to augment retirement income. The secret of productiveness of such a retirement plan is that the invested capital earns dividends not only all during the accumulation period, but also during the period when it is being drawn upon as a source of income."

An interesting withdrawal plan was offered by Hugh W. Long & Company early in 1957. The period over which payments will be made to the investor can be any specified number of years he selects, or may be extended for his lifetime. Amounts paid out depend primarily upon three things—the dollar total of investments made, changes in the value of shares bought month by month, and the length of time during which the withdrawal payments are to be made. The investor must remember that he may (and in most cases probably will) be eating into his principle if he wants fixed monthly payments of generous amounts; to give him those amounts, if they exceed the income on his plan for the period, shares and fractions of shares will have to be sold by the bank for his account to make up the number of dollars he wants.

Along the lines of the Teachers Insurance and Annuity Association insurance annuity plan, which combined with the CREF mentioned above offers protection against both inflation and deflation, Investors Diversified Services created in June, 1957, an Investors Variable Payment Fund, investing primarily in common stocks with emphasis on growth, to provide for automatic reinvestment of dividends and a variable payout of capital and income to the shareholder by periodic redemption of shares for an elected number of years. This new offering, with its equity investment feature, is designed to protect against inflation, while in conjunction with it the sponsor offers face amount installment certificates issued by Investors Syndicate of America, a fixed-dollar amount investment.

Another area in which broadened public interest has developed since 1953 is that of Canadian investment companies. Investing in Canada through these funds, rather than by direct purchase of Canadian shares, provides tax advantages to the U. S. investor. The funds do not distribute (they reinvest) dividends, and shareholders are not subject to U. S. income taxes. When you sell your shares, providing they have been held more than six months, the only U. S. tax is now limited to 25% on the capital gain which may be realized. At the end of 1957, eight of these Canadian companies were managing more than $320 million and serving some 125,000 U. S. shareholders.

In addition to Canada General Fund, Ltd., mentioned in the first edition of this book, others of the nature described above are:

Axe-Templeton Growth Fund of Canada

Canadian Fund

Canadian International Growth Fund

Investors Group Canadian Fund

Keystone Fund of Canada

N. Y. Capital Fund of Canada

Scudder Fund of Canada

United Funds Canada

One more new development since 1953 was the exploring by investment company distributors of the possibility of tax-free mutual funds. The basic idea was this: if a fund held nothing but tax-free securities, why should the income it passed along to its shareholders be taxable? Scenting a new market for shares among people interested in non-taxable income, and a broadened market for municipal bonds through possible creation of tax-free mutual funds, various interests proposed legislation favoring such funds. In 1955, 1956 and 1957 President Eisenhower expressed approval of this idea, but the bills introduced on their behalf (HR 8810, 8811 and 8812) met hard going in Congress.

The Bills are still pending, although new support has recently come into the picture and there may yet be tax-free mutual funds. Your dealer can tell you. At least four such funds, probably more, have been placed in registration with SEC awaiting enabling legislation.

With increasing numbers of investors in the United States, the question often arises: "Is it permissible to register securities directly in the name of a minor child?" If you are interested in giving some stock to a minor, you may wish to ask your investment dealer to get you a copy of *Stock Gifts To Minors,* prepared by the New York Stock Exchange and covering the subject in detail.

The George Putnam Fund, in the Winter 1957 edition of its *Prudent Investor,* summarized the matter well, somewhat as follows:

If you live in Alaska, Hawaii or the District of Columbia, or any one of 40 States (your dealer can tell you which ones) you can legally give securities to minors and manage the property for them until they are twenty-one. Laws recently passed permit you to register securities in your own name (or in the name of an adult member of the minor's family) as a custodian for the minor. Any gifts so made are irrevocable and convey title to the minor. As the custodian you post no bond, receive no compensation and can resign at any time. You can use part or all of the income or principal for the support, education or benefit of the minor.

Why was so much effort made to enact these laws? Mainly because they now make it easier for parents and grandparents to give gifts of securities to minor children. They also permit certain tax savings for the donors. The income from the investment is taxable to the child, if at all, at a tax rate much lower than the donor's. Thus, an over-all income tax saving for the family results. There is also a chance that a saving may be made in estate taxes.

In 1957 American investors put $1.42 billion of new money into mutual fund shares. People are used to big figures these days, but consider how much money this is. Had you been alive in the year 1 A.D. and gone into business, with a capital of $1.42 billion you could have lost $1,000 each and every day including Leap Year and still have had money left. In fact, your $1,000 a day would last until some time in the year 3888. Of this new money put into mutual funds in 1957 a substantial part came from investors "getting rich a little at a time" through systematic investing plans.

Serving these and other fund stockholders, as well as the creators and distributors of mutual fund shares, is the National Association of Investment Companies, with headquarters at 61 Broadway, New York 6. The Association has continued to expand its public information service, as well as its assistance to the industry it represents. Its color film, "The Hope That Jack Built," is in general use in motion picture theatres and has been seen by more than one million viewers as part of regular programs. Copies in the 16mm size are available if your dealer wishes to show you the picture. Another visual aid available to your dealer from NAIC is a slide film in color titled "Investing With A Purpose." Narrated by John Cameron Swayze, this also may be had for use at your club or before any other interested group.

Testifying to the increasingly important part mutual funds are playing in the American economic scene, the 1957 Mutual Fund Sales Convention saw a new high in attendance (some 1,600 people from 41 states, Washington, D. C., Canada and Hawaii) as well as a record number of exhibits. In addition to six displays · by related services there were exhibits by sponsors originating 69 nationally distributed mutual funds.

In making the closing address at the Convention, SEC Commissioner Andrew Downey Orrick reminded his hearers that "protection has been given to the investing public by providing prospective investors with adequate and reliable information about the management, finances and policies of investment companies," which, he said, "have become an impressively dynamic force among financial institutions," adding that "The general welfare of the American economy has been fostered by the resurgence of investment companies to public investment favor."

You, Mr., Mrs. or Miss Reader, probably have a drawer (or perhaps a safe desposit box) full of Uncle Sam's War Bonds or his Savings Bonds. You are his creditor. Perhaps you would like to become his partner, too, as you can do by investing in the securities which represent his free enterprise system. If you are considering mutual funds as a convenient way to do this, you will find these three facts of interest:

1. Mutual funds offer you from three to ten times the diversification of the Dow Jones Industrial Average, plus automatic supervision.

2. If you listed the 20 companies in the United States having the largest numbers of shareholders, you would find that four of them are mutual funds.

3. When you invest in a mutual fund, you are buying the only stock you will never have to change.

Index

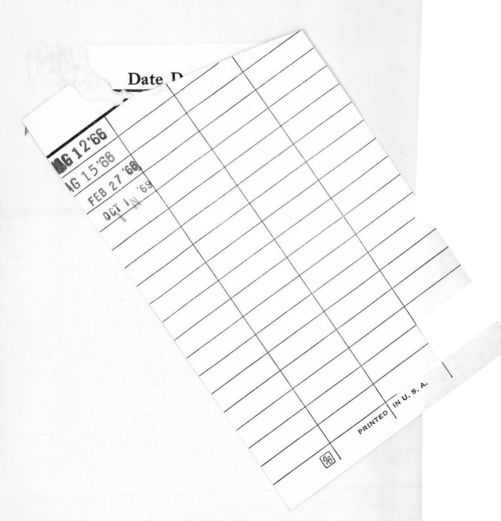

Date D

AG 12'66

AG 15'66

FEB 27 '68

OCT 1 N '69

PRINTED IN U.S.A.